THE NEWSPAPER EVERYTHING BOOK

VIVIENNE EISNER and ADELLE WEISS

The Newspaper Everything Book

How to make 150 useful objects
from old newspapers

A Sunrise Book | E. P. Dutton & Co., Inc. | New York | 1975

The items in this book are primarily the inventions of the authors. However, several derive from our common heritage and from the work of those before us who used newspapers as a good and serviceable material.

Photographs by Marshall Henrichs. Drawings by Adelle Weiss.

Dutton-Sunrise, Inc., a subsidiary of E. P. Dutton & Co., Inc.
First Edition
10   9   8   7   6   5   4   3

Published simultaneously in Canada by
Clarke, Irwin & Company Limited, Toronto and Vancouver

Library of Congress Cataloging in Publication Data

Eisner, Vivienne.
    The newspaper everything book.

    "A Sunrise book."
    Includes index.
    1. Paper work.   2. Newsprint.   I. Weiss, Adelle, joint author.   II. Title.
TT870.E36 1975   745.54   75–19145
ISBN 0–87690–179–8

CONTENTS

THE NEWSPAPER EVERYTHING BOOK

If yesterday's newspaper is still around the house, don't throw it away. This book will show you how to use it in any of a hundred different ways.

If you need a pair of *slippers* but can't see your way to spending the money on them just now, you needn't wait—make a fine pair from yesterday's newspaper.

If you're a teacher and your order for drawing and construction paper has been canceled—use newspapers.

If you don't like to buy expensive toys and games for your children—make some out of newspapers.

If you're living in a summer cottage or other temporary quarters and could use a few household items, make a *wastebasket,* a *broom,* or *curtains*—all from newspapers.

If you're a student without a desk *lamp,* make one out of newspapers—and have the pleasure of putting it together too.

At first, we were as skeptical as you may be. But as we worked and experimented with newspapers—creasing, crushing, compressing, rolling, folding, pleating, taping, and stapling—we discovered that well-designed newspaper products have durability, strength, and aesthetic appeal.

An object need not be massive to be strong. Taking their cue from bees, designers of aircraft learned to make honeycomb structures that are both lightweight and strong. In the same way, newspapers when folded and rolled in certain ways will support a heavy weight.

Try this simple experiment: Form a triangle from a folded strip of newspaper and staple closed. It supports a weight a hundred times its own.

You can understand why this principle works for the *table* and the *hanging shelf.* Newspapers can also be woven (see *baskets*), can withstand rain and snow (see *trellis* and *mat*), can hold water (see *containers*), and can be used to make garments and hats (see *halter* and *cap*).

Newspaper has many advantages over other types of paper—or cloth or other materials. It is abundant and available to everybody; you can even get it for free. Newspapers are available in nice, large sheets, and the columns of text provide a convenient grid for creasing and cutting. They are flexible but not flimsy, lightweight yet strong, permeable to air and water, and biodegradable.

But—you may be thinking—aren't newspapers extremely messy, flammable, ugly, and unmanageable? Wrong!—on every count!

When you work with newspapers, your hands do not get nearly as dirty as you might expect. If you use "fresh" newspaper, you will probably pick up more ink on your hands than if you work with a paper a week or so old. Other factors—how much you perspire, the time of year, and weather conditions—can make a difference. In any case, soap and water will easily remove the ink from your hands. We experienced no ill effects from this work, as a matter of fact, it seems to keep our hands strong and supple.

How permanent are newspaper products? An article in the *National Fisherman* (August 1974) tells of a sailboat made from newspaper and Aerolite, a synthetic resin adhesive. After twelve years of use this 17½-foot boat was still sound, seaworthy, and sailing. Even without exceptional measures, such as coating with epoxy, newspaper items can be used for a long time. A newspaper *shelf* bearing heavy plants has been hanging in a sunny window for six months and still shows no sign of deterioration. We tested the *mat* (p. 76) for months during the peak of last winter's snows, left it outdoors at the doorway, where it was subjected to both the elements and rubbing by many booted feet. It was still in good shape by the spring thaw, when we finally put it into the box for recycling. When summer came, we had similar good results with a test *rod* used as a plant stake in the garden. It stood up to a heavy rainy season, held up the tomato plant that was attached to it, and was not removed from the ground until early fall, along with the plant.

What about the fire hazard associated with products made from newspaper? Newspapers require no more attention in handling than the fabrics, plastics, and other flammable material we have learned to use with care in all areas of daily living. As a matter of fact, if you roll a *log for burning* (p. 73) without sufficient air space between the layers of newspaper, the log will not burn, under ordinary conditions. And if you want to fireproof a newspaper product, you can apply the same spray used to fireproof

Christmas trees. There are also fire retardants for cellulosic materials, such as newspaper, that rely on impregnation with solutions or water suspensions of salts, such as borax, boric acid, sodium calcium borate, ammonium sulfate, or ammonium phosphate.

How much time is required for a project? In general, simple projects like the *sunglasses* take only a few minutes; the *thick-soled sandals* take about an hour (but they will be useful for a long time); and even a large object like the *table* can be completed in a couple of hours or less. In fact, you can make the rolls for its construction while watching the nightly news on TV. You may want to experiment or make changes in an item. And we've found it's so much fun that the question, How long does it take? doesn't arise.

Is more than one person needed on any project? Everything can be made alone; however, a large structure like the *beach umbrella* is easier and faster to construct with the help of another person. Also, making things from newspapers turns out to be a great family and friendly venture. We have even had several Newspaper Happenings in our homes.

How can you vary the look of the objects you make? The appearance of a product depends, among other things, on the choice of newspaper, for example, black and white or color; text or photo; front page or stock quotations; English or foreign language. What could be more appropriate at a children's party than hats made out of the Sunday comics? And Chinese newspapers make attractive fans. Other decorative touches can be added by curling, pleating, and collage. Newspapers also provide an excellent surface for wax, tempera, plastic, paint, and varnish (bucket, p. 30). Besides the visual effects of such coatings, they can make the product more durable. And good workmanship counts too in making an aesthetically pleasing item.

The ecological benefits of reusing newspapers are obvious. The Forest Service of the U.S. Dept. of Agriculture reports that one Sunday issue of a large metropolitan newspaper may consume all the pulpwood from seventy-five acres of average forest. That's a lot of trees for a commodity that you read once and ordinarily throw away! And twenty-five tons of recycled newspaper saves 4000 trees!

So this book is an invitation to stop looking at a newspaper as a one-time thing to read and throw away. We ask you to share the discoveries we have made in the uses of this available resource. Our instructions give you the fundamentals. But they are only guides, and you may find yourself improving some of our methods and even inventing new uses.

11

The following basic terms and units of construction are really very simple and are put to use over and over again. Once you become familiar with them, you should have no difficulty in following the directions for making the products that interest you.

Keep a kit of scissors, masking tape, glue, and a stapler handy.

At times, you will also use a hole punch, paperclips, paper fasteners, pins, rubber bands, bag ties, string, yarn, and a needle and thread.

As shown below, a sheet is two pages, or a full double spread.

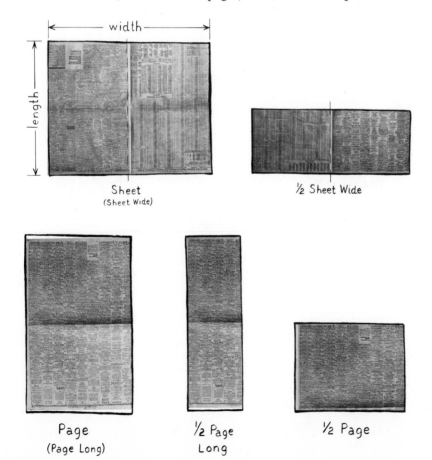

Sheet
(Sheet Wide)

½ Sheet Wide

Page
(Page Long)

½ Page
Long

½ Page

Unless otherwise noted, by *newspapers* we mean those of ordinary, large-size format; *tabloid* refers to a small-size newspaper.

For good-looking and well-constructed products, line up newspapers evenly for cutting, folding, and putting together. Also, when folding, be sure to press the folds firmly.

In the process of making newsprint, the wood pulp falls into a direction, or grain. It is easier to tear newspaper the long way, with the grain, rather than across the width.

3 Sheets Together

Sheets Together

By this term, we mean the laying of sheets on top of each other, with edges aligned, so that they can be used as one.

This improves strength and can provide thickness where needed.

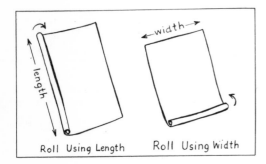

Roll Using Length   Roll Using Width

Plain Roll

Roll newspaper along the length or width as needed. It's best to start a roll by first folding the newspaper in half.

Tape the roll closed with a piece of tape at each end and in the middle.

You can also flatten a roll to use as a strip.

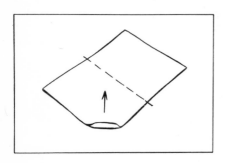

Diagonal Roll

Hold newspaper at an angle. Start at one corner and roll.

Tape closed in as many places as needed to keep the parts of a unit together—around each end and in the middle.

Rod

Roll a sheet (or two together) tightly.

Tape closed at both ends and in the middle.

Flatten the roll, then crease down the center and tape closed again, this time wrapping the tape around tightly to keep the sides together. Use five or more strips of tape to do this, depending upon the length of the rod.

Tape and/or glue two rods together for added strength.

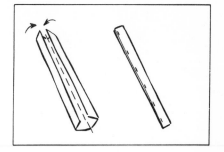

Straight-Folded Flat Strip

A folded flat strip can be made from any size piece of newspaper.

Fold the paper in half. Fold the sides in toward the center to the desired width of the strip. Use as is or close with tape, glue, or staples.

Diagonal Flat Strip

Holding newspaper at an angle, fold sides in first; then fold into a strip, sides in toward the center.

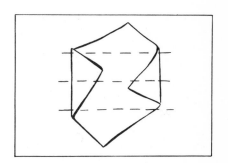

This makes a more flexible strip than the straight-folded flat strip.

Disk

Use flat or diagonal strips. Start winding at one end to form the center; continue to wind the rest of the strip around itself. Staple, tape, or glue the tailend to the outside of the disk. To make the disk larger, tape another strip to the outside and continue winding.

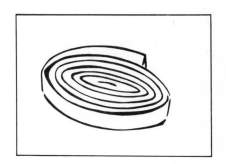

Overlapping

This is another way to put sheets together for additional thickness or length.

As you place one layer of newspaper on top of another, leave a few inches overhang at one end.

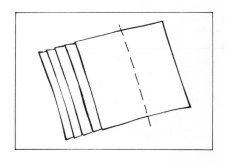

Crushing

Take a piece of newspaper and gather it into a ball. Then open it up and smooth it out. Repeat three or four times until the newspaper is softened. Use a single layer or two to three layers together, either plain or glued.

15

Compressing

Compressing restores some of the characteristics of the wood pulp from which newspapers are made. This means that when a tight roll of newspaper is pressed into a fold and taped closed, it can be used in similar ways to wood. Compressing is also achieved by pressing many layers of newspaper together and taping as tightly as possible.

In addition to glue and tape, nails and screws can be used to hold compressed-paper items together.

Finishing

To enhance the surface of a piece, paint it with plastic paint, either directly or over an undercoat of gesso or modeling paste. Finishing makes the item stronger as well as more conventionally decorative.

Insertion Closure

Beginning with a folded piece, you make an insertion closure by slipping one end into the opening of the other side.

Laminating

Laminating makes the newspaper firm and as sturdy as lightweight cardboard. Glue two or more layers of newspaper together with rubber cement, white glue, or a mixture of half water and half glue.

Pleating

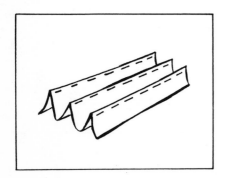

Newspapers can be pleated easily.

To stiffen pleats, tape along the ends of each pleat or staple each pleat near the fold, as shown.

You can also make a strip by pleating a page or sheet. Fold the last section around the pleating and staple closed. Result: a strong, flexible strip.

Slotting

To make a slot at a fold, sew or staple a seam about ½ to 1 inch in from the edge of the fold. This forms a place in which to insert a roll or rod.

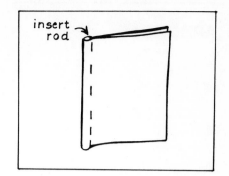

Stapling To Shape

After you have formed a shape by creasing or folding, staple close to the creased edges to keep the shape.

Wrapping

Wind strips (plain or crushed) around an inner core for strength. For a smooth outer surface, wrap with a single layer of newspaper.

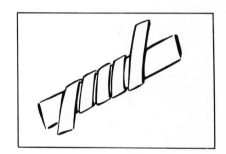

APRONS

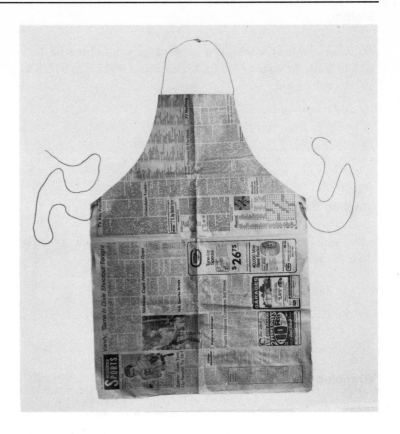

BASIC APRON

Put three *sheets* together.

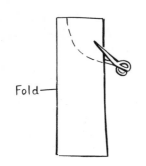

Fold in half the long way and cut an arc from the outer corner at the top, as shown.

Open. Fold the top edges down about 1 inch.

Center a piece of yarn (about 20 inches long) inside the fold and tape the fold closed. Tie the ends of the yarn together so that the loop slips easily over your head.

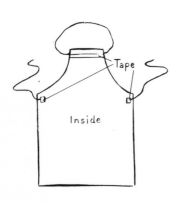

Punch a hole on each side at the waist. Through the holes put strings long enough to tie around your waist. To keep the strings firmly in place, tape over at the holes.

Add pockets if desired.

When your newspaper apron gets dirty (as all aprons eventually do), throw it away and make a new one.

WORK APRON

Put two *sheets* together and fold in half to page size (four layers).

Crease the folded edge up about a third of the way. This will form the pockets. Staple on each side and in the middle. Make holes in the sides near the top. Put through yarn ties long enough to tie around your waist. Tape over the holes to keep the yarn securely in place.

BALL AND BAT

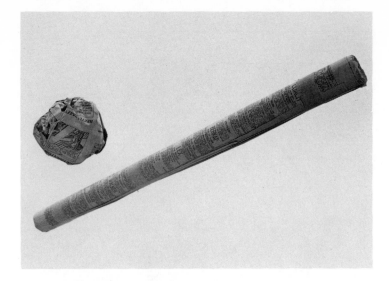

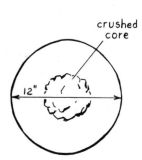

crushed core

12"

Crush a *page* of newspaper and form it into a tight, round shape. Wrap tape around this core so that it will stay firm. Place it in the center of a second page and crumple this second piece around the core, shaping the covered core with your hands as if it were a ball of clay. Crisscross some tape around the ball. Repeat until you have the size ball you want.

For a neat cover, cut a round piece of newspaper. For the ball pictured, which measures 12 inches in circumference, a circle with a 12-inch diameter was used. Place the rounded crushed-paper core in the middle, fold, and tape closed.

Put twelve *sheets* together and fold to page size. Starting at the fold, roll, and tape closed. Make the roll tight for a strong, hard bat.

To add a neat cover, place the roll at one end of a folded sheet of newspaper and roll it in the paper as snugly as possible. Tape the cover closed in at least three places.

PLAITED BASKET

Here is a basket that is easy to make, flexible, and lightweight. It is useful for picnics and to hold various small items. And it can be used as an Easter basket or a party or gift basket.

Make eight 1½-inch-wide strips each folded from the length of a *page* and three 1½-inch-wide strips each folded from the width of a full *sheet*.

Closely interweave the eight strips, as shown, to make the bottom of the basket.

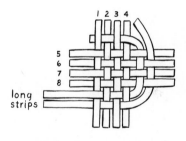

Weave two of the longer strips around the outside, bringing up and forming the sides of the basket. Tape the ends of the strips together.

To finish the basket, place the third long strip over the top edges. Staple the strip to the top as you go along, and to close it, insert one end into the other and staple.

"REED" BASKET

The reed basket is sturdy and long-lasting. Depending on the size you want, make two or three diagonal strips for the base. The basket shown is made with three diagonal strips as a base, each made from a *sheet*.

Wind the strips into a disk, adding a little glue here and there as you go. To complete the base, make a straight strip 1½ inches wide from a *page* folded to half-page size. Wrap this around the

disk keeping it in place with a little glue. The open side faces up to hold the upright rolls for weaving.

Make sixteen tight rolls, each from a *page* folded to half-page size. Tape closed. Insert and glue them into the strip, spacing them evenly around the base.

Make five narrow diagonal strips, each from a *page*. Make four 1½-inch-wide regular strips, each from a *sheet*.

Weave the strips in and out of the rolls, alternating the diagonal strips with the regular strips. Use one strip for each row. Cut to the right length. Tape the ends together on the inside of the basket.

Upside down, use as a stand for a plant. Using a larger base and longer rolls, make a laundry basket.

outer strip

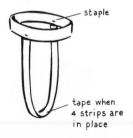

staple

tape when
4 strips are
in place

WOVEN BASKET

Because this basket is deep and has an open weave, it is especially useful as a small hamper to hold a few soiled clothes. It's a good wastebasket, holds 5 pounds of apples, and can serve as a catchall for a child's toys. You may want to keep socks or other items in it to separate them on a closet shelf.

Use a *sheet* folded to half-page size to make a strip about 2 inches wide. Staple ends together to form a ring.

Using a *sheet* folded to page size for each, make nine page-length strips, each about 1 inch wide.

Insert the ends of four of these strips inside the fold of the ring and staple in place, each strip going from one side of the ring to the point opposite, as shown. Arrange strips evenly, and when all are in place, tape at the bottom to keep them centered.

Weave each of the remaining five strips in and out of this frame and staple each strip's ends together. The bottom of the basket is rounded until placed on a hard surface. To line the bottom, press in a single *page* folded into quarters.

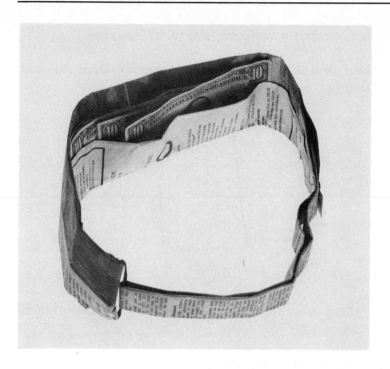

Fold a *sheet* to page size. Fold in half again along the length. Turn about 2 inches on each side in toward the center.

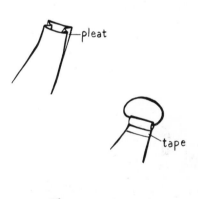

About 3½ inches from one end make a tuck on each side to taper this end.

Place a thick rubber band over this tapered end, fold about 1 inch of the end over the rubber band, and tape the folded piece down. The rubber band makes the belt adjustable to your size.

To taper the other end of the belt, cut triangular pieces on each side, leaving the end about two inches wide. Open the two layers of the cut tapered end and tape around the edge of each layer separately. Punch aligned holes through both layers.

Make a straight narrow strip from half a *page* and fold in half. Put this strip through the rubber band; punch holes as shown. Insert the strip into the other end of the belt. A brad through the holes will hold the belt closed.

BIB

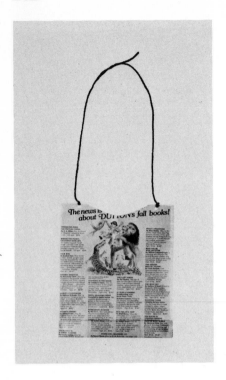

Use one *sheet* of newspaper folded to half-page size.

Fold along *A* and cut neck opening as shown. Open and punch holes to attach yarn or string.

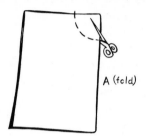

A (fold)

Fold up about 1½ inches at bottom of bib. Tape sides to form pocket.

Make a new bib for every meal, or as necessary.

Bibs can be made larger for adults who enjoy eating lobster.

"BAMBOO" BLIND

Make tight rolls using two tabloid *sheets* folded to page size for each roll. The number of rolls will vary according to the size of your window. Tape each roll closed at both ends and in the middle.

Make five ½-inch-wide strips, each from a crushed tabloid *page*.

Lay out the finished rolls one next to the other. Weave the strips over and under each roll. Dab some glue on each strip to keep it in place on the rolls. Let dry.

To hang the blind, make two 1-inch-wide strips, each from half a tabloid *page*. Make each into a ring and staple its ends together. Slip a ring on each end of the top roll before you have completed weaving with the ½-inch strips.

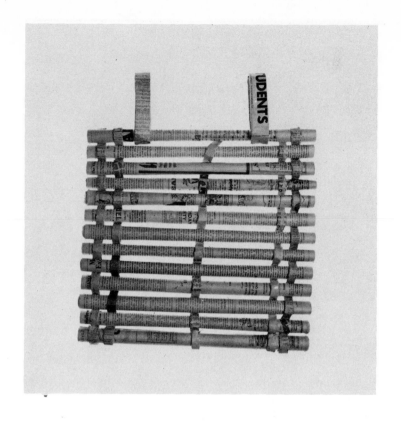

For a durable, decorative bookcover, use a single *page* of newspaper for each book.

Make a thin paste of flour and water. Brush the paste on the paper. Then paint with watercolors or inks while the paste is still wet. You can create a textured design by moving your fingers, a comb, or other tool gently through the painted surface.

Let dry. Rub surface lightly with a wax candle. This provides a protective coating.

Center the open book on the unfinished side of the page. Fold down the top of the newspaper cover, fold up the bottom, and fold the ends toward the center to fit the size of the book. Slip the front and back covers of the book into the folded ends.

BOOKCOVER

25

BOOKEND

Put five *sheets* together. Fold to half-page size to form a long, heavy strip. Tape the long side closed. Bend the strip in half. Squeeze one end a bit to open up a pocket.

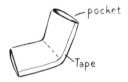

Fold four *sheets* to half-page size. Fold lengthwise twice more. Tape closed. Bend in half and insert one half inside the pocket of the first strip.

The half left on the outside functions as the end support and serves as a pocket for supporting rods.

Make five rods, each from a *sheet* folded to half-page size. Fold each rod in half. Insert two rods into the pocket, one on each side of the support. Put the remaining three rods into the pocket of the outside support. This adds weight and strength to the bookend.

Fold two *sheets* of newspaper together to page size and roll into a hollow tube. Tape closed at both ends and in the middle. But don't tape *over* the ends; leave them open to receive the ends of the rod.

Fold a *page* to half-page size, roll tightly into a rod, and tape closed.

Crease the hollow tube in two places to form a base. Bend the rod and insert each end into the appropriate open end of the hollow tube to make a triangular structure.

Two of these are needed to support a book. By raising or lowering the bent rods, the bookrest can adjust to different size books.

To protect your open book from dirt or spills, you can put clear plastic around it before placing it in the bookrest.

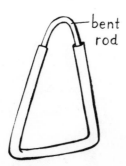

bent rod

BOX WITH COVER

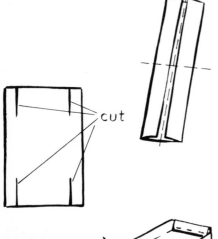

Fold a *sheet* to page size. Fold the long sides to the center, then spread glue over top half and fold down.

Make creases about 1¼ inches in from the long sides and make four 3-inch cuts as shown.

This gives you two short strips and a flap between at each end. Bring the two strips together and staple closed. Fold the flap up and over the stapled strips and staple again.

To make a cover that slips over the box, fold a *page* to half-page size. Make an insertion closure, tucking in about 2 inches. Staple closed. Tuck corners as shown, fold over, and staple closed. Make tucks at the open end, insert box, fold down edge, and close with paperclips.

If you make one box slightly larger than another, the pair can nest, or the larger box can be used as a cover for the smaller.

Carry your sandwiches for lunch, your tubes of oil paint—anything you want to protect or keep together. Make the box to fit your needs.

BRACKET

Make a diagonal strip from two *sheets* together. Fold in the center and shape into a triangle, bending so that the top of the bracket measures 5 inches and the back 4 inches. This gives you overlapping ends, which you tape together to retain the shape. To reinforce the bottom, wind a strip made from a diagonal roll (made from a *sheet*) around it.

Hang the bracket with string between two nails or screws.

Holds about 5 pounds weight. To use for hanging plants, tie a loop of string to the end of the bracket.

BROOM

You need twelve rods. Make each rod from a *sheet* folded to page size. Tape the twelve rods together at one end.

To add a broom handle, take twelve *sheets* together folded to page size, roll tightly, and tape closed. Tape the twelve rods around and onto one end of the handle.

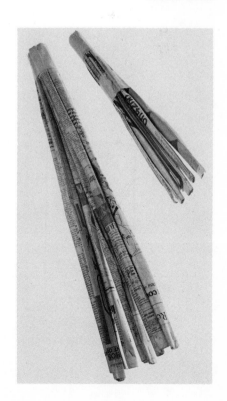

For a whisk broom, use twelve rods, each made from a *page* of newspaper that has been folded in half.

These are long-lasting, handy brooms to use indoors and out.

BUCKET

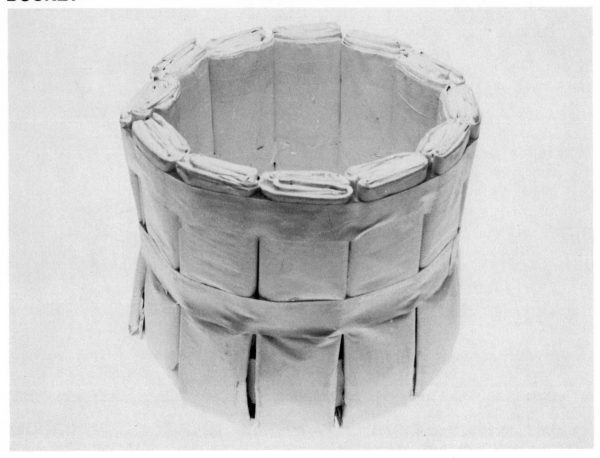

The bucket consists of three parts: base, side sections, and support ring.

For the base, make nine or ten diagonal strips, using a *sheet* for each. Form into a disk. As you add one strip onto the next and shape into a disk, use a little glue to make firm.

Twelve sections are needed for the sides. Make each section from a *sheet* as follows:

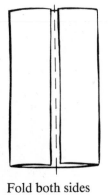

Fold both sides
in toward the center.

Fold down
in half.

Fold in
half again.

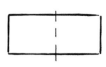

Fold into thirds, open
edges on the inside.

Fold in half the other way.

Tape closed around the middle and toward the open end, leaving an opening, or loop, at the fold.

Tape

When the twelve sections are completed, make a long straight strip about 1½ inches wide from a *sheet*.

Thread this strip through the loops of the twelve side sections. Join the sections, touching, in a circle.

strip

Using three long, straight strips, each about 1 inch wide, and each made from a *sheet,* make a support ring to fit inside the outer rim of the bottom of the bucket. Wind around about four times. Glue in place.

On top of this, glue the base.

Also spread a little glue around to hold the side sections to the base.

Tape around the outside of the bucket in the center and toward the top.

The bucket shown in the photograph has been painted with latex paint.

BUILDING BLOCK

Fold ten *sheets* together in half along the full width of the newspaper.

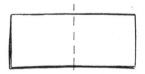

Fold in half twice again. Press folds firmly and tape together in several places.

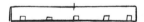

Make a second unit in the same way.

Fold and interlock both units so that the folds and edges alternate.

BUILDING UNITS

Tape together compactly, as shown.

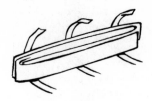

Make another section of two units.

If you want, you can add glue between the two sections before taping them together.

Tape the two sections together, compressing them as tightly as possible by wrapping the tape around a couple of times.

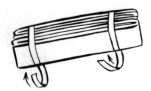

For each segment of the building block you need two sections.

You can make a building block of eight segments arranged as shown, leaving a hollow core. Or if you prefer, make the block solid, with another segment in the center.

Hold together with glue between the segments and tape around the full cube.

This is a heavy, sturdy block, suitable for a seat, step-stool, bookshelf supports, and similar purposes.

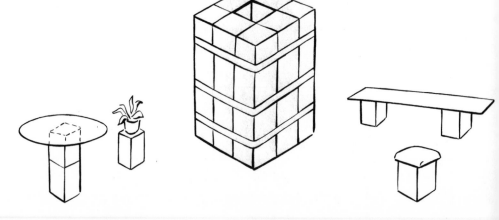

BUILDING BRICK

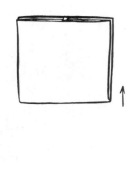

1. For each brick, begin with four *sheets*. Fold the outside edges to the center.

2. Fold up in half.

3. Then twice more.

4. Fold in half again.

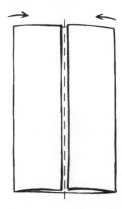

5. Make a second section. Insert one side of the second section into the fold of the first and tape both together tightly to form one set.

6. Compress two sets (four sections) together tightly. Tape to make one brick.

Each brick consists of 512 layers of paper under compression.

You can glue a single strip of paper over the tape bands for a neater effect.

Stack bricks to use as supports for bookshelves. Use as you would regular bricks, holding them together with tape and glue instead of mortar.

CARRIER

Use a *sheet* folded to page size. Fold down in half twice; then fold to the side in half. Tape side edges together on the outside.

Bring taped edges to center. Press folds firmly.

Open to form box shape.

Make six of these. Tape together in two rows of three each.

Make seven strips 4 inches wide, each from a *half-sheet wide* width.

Place the six sections on top of two strips going the long way and three strips going the short way. Bring up the ends of the strips, fold them over the top edges into the boxes, and staple them to the sides of the sections.

For the handle, use three *sheets* together folded to page size. Make a 1-inch-wide strip. Wrap with another strip made from a *half-sheet wide* folded to a 2-inch strip. Tape the handle in place. Wrap the outside with a *sheet* folded to a 6-inch strip. Tape closed.

Use the last two 4-inch-wide strips to wrap around under the bottom and up each side of the end sections, as shown. Tuck in and staple to the sides.

Use to carry cleaning aids. The compartments are big enough for quart-size liquid cleaners. Also handy for carrying tools and art supplies.

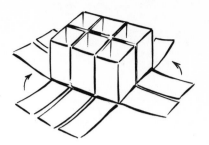

Put three *sheets* together.

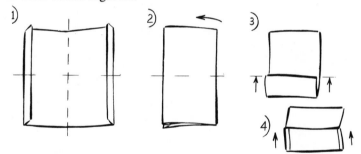

CASE

1. Fold in about 2 inches on each side toward the center. (Fold in more for a smaller case.)

2. Fold in half lengthwise.

3. Bring the bottom up to the center line.

4. Fold again. Staple and tape the sides.

The case shown has a glued-on cover made from newspaper chosen for its attractive appearance.

Tuck a case inside your pocketbook, briefcase, or traveling bag. Good for holding cosmetics, papers, and small items; also for separating items, such as dirty laundry, in your luggage.

CHECKERS
(AND DECKERS)

You can make a checkerboard and checkers to play checkers or a similar game called deckers (see instructions below).

To make the board, cut a piece of laminated (three layers) newspaper into an 8-inch square. Paste plain paper to cover one surface. Cut thirty-two 1-inch squares from the comics. Paste each in its appropriate place on the plain surface.

For the checkers, cut twenty-four 1-inch circles from a laminated (five layers) straight strip. Make twelve circles with a final cover of plain paper on both surfaces, the remaining twelve with paper from the comics pasted on both surfaces. Color a dot on one side of each circle to denote a king.

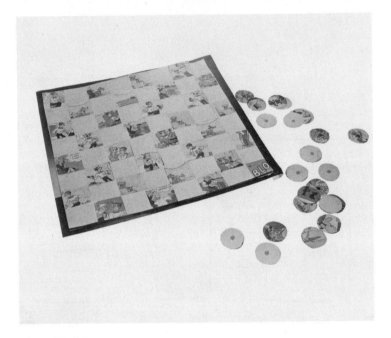

DECKERS*

To play deckers, set up the board as you do for checkers. Men are moved and jumped in the same way except that they are not removed from the board when they are jumped. Instead, when you jump your opponent, you take his decker along, placing it under yours. As the game progresses, stacks of two or more deckers develop, sometimes intermixed. The stack belongs to the top decker and is moved as a unit. But when a stack is jumped, only its top decker is taken along under the jumper. Kings are made the same as in checkers (turn the decker over to show the king dot) and have the same privileges as in checkers. All possible jumps must be taken. When all the other players' deckers are covered by yours, you win.

* Invented by Leonard Eisner. Copyright pending.

The chess pieces are made from pleated strips of different widths.

For the king and queen, use a 3-inch-wide pleated strip folded from a single-*page long*.

Make pawns from a ¾-inch-wide pleated strip from a *page long*.

For the remaining pieces, use a 1½-inch-wide pleated strip from a *page long*.

Pleat each strip to within 2 inches of the end. Use this end piece to wrap around the pleated strip to enclose and cover it. Tape closed.

Identify the chess pieces by means of curled, folded, and cut pieces that slip between pleats on the top of the chess pieces. Color half of the set black.

Make the chessboard the same as the *checkerboard*. Use 2-inch instead of 1-inch squares to accommodate the larger playing pieces.

CHRISTMAS TREE DECORATIONS

Form straight strips in a variety of widths made from a tabloid *sheet* or *page* into sturdy and attractive hanging decorations. Bend or twist the strips into different shapes—rectangles, triangles, circles. Glue the ends together and tape the ornament on a narrow strip for hanging.

Make a wreath base from twisted diagonal rolls.

Use tines (see under *comb*) to make a star. Cover the center, front, and back, with specially selected newspaper.

Use curled, twisted, pleated, or fringed newspaper to enhance the surface of any shape.

Quickly and easily, fashion festoons from diagonally cut single strips of paper. Pleat the strips at an angle, making one side deeper than the other. This allows the strip to curve gracefully. Glue or tape the strips together. Use to drape and trim a tree, window, or doorway.

You can base classroom projects on almost every product and suggested use of newspapers in this book. Here we direct your attention to a few that students of all ages particularly enjoy doing.

The jewelry, ties, buckles, and belts, worn as costume accessories, offer lots of opportunity for fanciful decorative treatment.

The toy furniture shown is one form of model-making with laminated newspapers. The medium is excellent for this purpose; it holds its shape when cut and folded like lightweight cardboard, but unlike cardboard it doesn't crack when folded and is easy to cut. Also, newspaper columns serve as a good guide for making straight-line cuts without using a ruler. All sorts of models are possible: large-scale airplanes to hang from the ceiling, castles, boats, and urban-planning layouts.

When lesson plans are disrupted, the movie you've planned doesn't arrive, or the children are restless, a stack of newspapers, some tape, and a supply of scissors will save the day!

JEWELRY

Make finger rings and earrings from small disks rolled from narrow straight strips.

Use narrow straight strips to make a necklace. Fold in the same way as for *kindling bricks.*

Make bracelets from strips too. Wrap with narrow strips to decorate and make them sturdy.

NECKTIES

Laminate three *pages*. Trace a necktie shape plus 2 inches more at the top. Cut out. Fold and tape down the tab in the back. Make a ½-inch strip, slip through the tab, and fasten under your collar with a brad.

Make a bow tie from a single layer of newspaper, 4 by 6 inches. Fold in half and make cuts as shown. Fold the tabs to the back, trim, and tape closed to form a slot. Slip a ½-inch strip through the tab. Fasten with a brad.

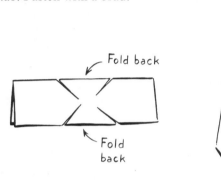

TOY FURNITURE

Laminate three or four *pages* together and cut as necessary. Bend, fold, staple, tape, and glue to suit your designs. The furniture in the photograph was cut as shown in the drawing.

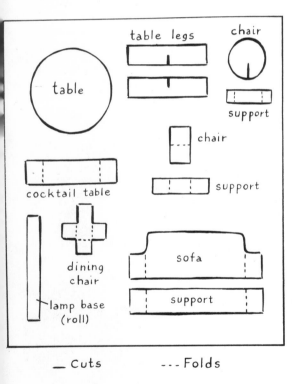

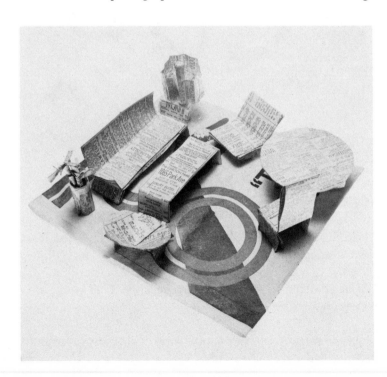

BELT

A belt can be made from straight strips, but for a more flexible sash, use diagonal strips. Use one *sheet* and add sheets as needed to create the length of belt desired.

BUCKLE

Use a 1-inch-wide straight strip made from a *page long*.

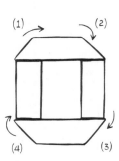

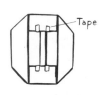

1. Fold strip in front at right angles.

2. Then fold down in back at right angles.

3. Forward again.

4. Fold up in back at right angles.

Cut off excess. Tape strip closed.

Roll a cross piece from a small piece of paper. Cut to fit buckle. Insert into open sides of strip and tape in place.

A good buckle to wrap with yarn to go with a handmade yarn belt.

CLIP

Make a rod from a *page* folded to half-page size. Bend the rod in half and tape the halves firmly together near the bend. Wrap a rubber band around the clip near the open ends for additional tension.

This clip is good for hanging wet paintings and prints because it does not mark the dampened paper. It works well over a wooden hanger to hold clothes in place, on a clipboard, and for training vines to a trellis.

COASTER

We have used these coasters to protect our furniture.

They are absorbent, flat, easy to make, and readily disposable.

For each coaster, use half a *page*.

Fold in half.

Then fold down into thirds.

Bring the folded edge over almost to the other edge. Tuck the leftover end into the opening. Crease sharply. Staple or tape closed if you want.

A comb you can throw away after one use can be handy for a person or animal with a contagious condition. Also useful for crafts, for spreading and making patterns in viscous material.

To make each tine, cut a single strip of paper about 3½ by 6 inches. Fold in half. On the folded side bring corners to the center to form a triangle.

Fold each side of the triangle in half toward the center again, and repeat.

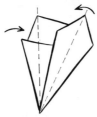

Bring sides together and tape closed. Trim top and tape closed.

Make as many additional tines as you need.

Cut another single strip of paper about 6 by 13 inches and fold down twice. Fold left edge toward center.

Lay tines across bottom. Tape evenly in place, leaving about 1 inch below bottom of backing. Fold over top. Staple closed.

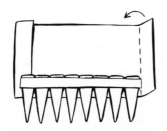

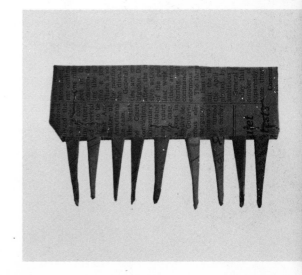

CONTAINERS

COILED CONTAINER

Roll six or more 1-inch-wide diagonal strips, each made from a *sheet* of newspaper.

Wind into a disk, adding one to the other. Use tape or glue to attach the strips.

When you have the size you want, push the middle down, telescoping the disk to form a container. Squeeze small amounts of glue into the folds of the strips so that the container will hold its shape.

The shape of this container lends itself well to a growing plant. It can be hung if you tie three cords onto the last strip before you glue it in place.

CONE-SHAPED CONTAINER

This is a favorite container for party candy and potato chips. If you need a quickly made container to gather berries, shells, or pine cones, here it is.

Fold a tabloid *page* to half-page size. Pinch the center at the folded edge and bring the sides around to form a cone shape. Tape closed.

To eliminate the open hole at the bottom, you can take one layer of paper from the top point, fold it back over the hole, and tape it to the opposite edge.

CONTAINER FOR LIQUID

Fold a *sheet* to half-page size; then fold down again. The folded edge is the top of the container.

Insert one side into the fold of the other. Staple closed. Flatten.

At the bottom of each side make a tuck. Hold the bottom edges together, fold up about 1 inch, and staple.

Tape all the way over the bottom and side, as shown.

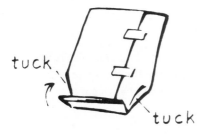

COSTUMES

The wig, three-cornered hat, ruffled jabot, and tiny glasses shown in the photograph can be used for the bicentennial celebration, school plays, and costume parties.

WIG

The wig is made from many pieces of curled paper glued onto a frame (see *three-cornered hat*).

JABOT

The jabot is made from four 2-inch-wide pieces of newspaper, gathered, and stapled one to the other to give a layered appearance.

SPECTACLES

For the spectacles, use a *page,* fold twice, and laminate the layers. Draw the pattern for the spectacles all in one piece; just fold the earpieces to fit over your ears.

You can make a great variety of costumes out of newspapers—king, queen, fairy princess, Indian, witch, ballet dancer, animals; hats, crowns, fringed skirts, beards, wigs, collars to represent a notable person or fantastic creature.

THREE-CORNERED HAT

Start by making a headband from a 2-inch-wide straight strip made from a *sheet* folded to page size. Wrap this around your head, overlap to fit, and fasten the ends together with staples or tape.

Make two 3-inch-wide strips, each from a *page* folded to half-page size. Put the ends of one strip into the headband so that the strip runs from front to back over the crown of your head. Fit it to your head size before you staple in place.

Cross the second strip over the first, put the ends into the head-band strip, and staple in place. The hat frame is now completed.

To make the brim, laminate three full *sheets*. Put the frame on the top sheet, in the middle, and trace around the headband. Cut out the center.

Draw the pattern for the brim, as shown, and cut.

Place the frame on top of the cutout section of the brim and tape the two parts together. Bring up the back and the sides of the brim and tape to the frame.

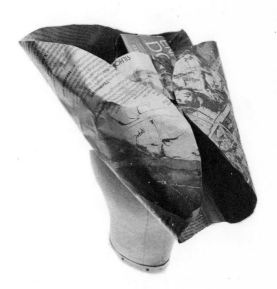

CROQUET MALLET AND WICKETS

To make the mallet handle, put five *sheets* together and fold to page size. Roll tightly and tape closed.

For the mallet head, fold a *sheet* to page size and make a 3-inch-wide straight strip. Roll up the strip loosely and tape closed. Make a hole in its top. Put glue on one edge of the handle and wedge it into the hole of the head.

For each wicket, roll about three or four *sheets* together. Tape closed. At each end attach a disk, each disk made from two diagonal strips.

Use with newspaper *balls* for indoor croquet.

CUBE

The cube is made of rolls, each roll composed of three *sheets* folded together to page size, rolled tightly, and taped closed.

Make three sides of fourteen rolls each. Glue and tape together two sets of three rolls each and two sets of four rolls each; then tape all fourteen rolls together.

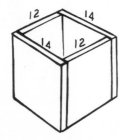

Make two sides of twelve rolls each. Glue and tape together three sets of four rolls each. Tape all twelve together.

To assemble, fit the two sides of twelve rolls each between two sides of fourteen rolls each. Glue together. Glue the third side with fourteen rolls on top.

Tape all around.

For reinforcement, make four shorter rolls, two 12 inches long and two 10 inches long. Glue these against the inside corners of the top of the cube.

A cube can be used in many ways—as a small table, for storage of magazines and records, or as a stand for plants and sculpture. Stacked cubes can be used by children for building.

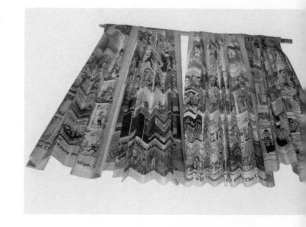

CURTAIN

If you need a temporary curtain in a dormitory room, camper, or other transient living quarters, these newspaper curtains offer a quick and attractive solution; and there is no need for sewing or spending time or money. In a basement, garage, or similar area, where these curtains are handy, they are easily replaced when dirty.

The curtain shown is made from a full sheet of newspaper, pleated, and taped onto a rod.

You can make curtains longer or wider by gluing sheets together. Curtains can be taped either directly onto the window frame or onto a curtain rod.

DOLL

For the head, crush a *page* into a round shape and place it in the center of another *page*. Gather the second page around the crushed core. Wrap the bottom edge with string to form a neck.

Make the body by folding a *page* to half-page size, and again widthwise. Make an insertion closure, tucking in about 1 inch. Glue or tape closed.

Put the head into the body. Tuck in the top corners of the body. Using yarn, sew the body onto the neck; stuff the body with crushed paper.

Fold a *sheet* to half-page size, and again widthwise, and roll. Tape or glue closed. Make three of these—two for the legs, one to use for both arms.

Dab glue onto the upper part of two rolls and insert them into the body for legs. Press the front and back of the body together and stitch between the legs with yarn. Center the remaining roll on the upper back and tape in place.

Cut and shape the ends of the rolls for feet and hands, gluing pieces of paper over the edges, as necessary.

Add features and hair; clothes can be made, too.

DUSTER

Fold ten *sheets* together to page size. Starting at the open edges, roll lengthwise. Fasten roll with tape. Make 6-inch cuts into the edges of the roll at one end. Make the cuts about ½ inch apart.

Use to dust furniture and plants.

DUSTPAN

Fold a *sheet* to page size. Fold each long edge in toward the center about 2 inches. Fold in half by bringing up the bottom edge; then turn in the sides as shown and staple closed. Roll the top down; staple the layers of the roll inside. Crease the bottom fold well. If you want a sharper edge, trim it with tape.

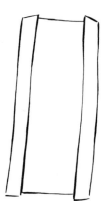  

EMBROIDERY HOOP

Use a *sheet* to make a diagonal roll. Roll as tightly as possible. Flatten.

Form into a circle about 6½ inches in diameter. The overlapped ends are taped in place.

Make a straight strip about 1¼ inches wide from a *half-page long*.

Cover the circle with the strip. Push the circle in toward the fold of the strip and staple the strip as close as possible to the bottom of the inner circle.

Use another *sheet* to make a diagonal roll, this one rolled not quite as tightly as the first. Flatten, and shape as closely as you can around the first hoop. Tape overlapped ends together.

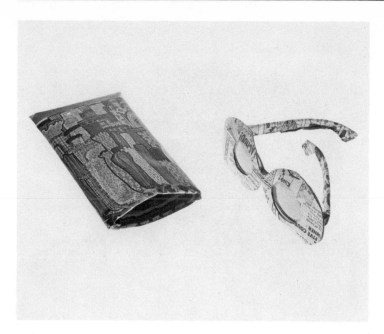

Fold a *sheet* to half-page size. Fold it in half the long way; open, then fold in 2 inches on each side.

Fold the top and bottom edges in about ½ inch and tape down. Bring the top and bottom edges together, tuck in the bottom corners, and tape the sides closed.

For a more attractive case, cover with specially selected newspaper.

FAN

In addition to the pleated fan that all schoolchildren make, you can construct a handsome folding fan.

Use two *sheets,* each folded to page size.

Pleat each folded sheet, using the width. Make the pleats ¾-inch.

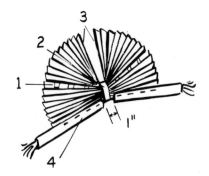

1. Tape the two sections together along one side.

2. Bring the pleats together and put tape around the center.

3. Bring edges together (at 3, as shown) and tape.

4. Make two 1½-inch-wide straight strips, each from a *page* folded to quarter-page size. Staple strips to edges. Leave 1 inch space in the middle.

Use decorative, specially selected newspaper.

Use four *sheets,* each folded to page size. Fold each diagonally pressing the fold from corner to corner.

Lay out evenly, one on top of the other, with about 3-inch spaces between. Tape in place.

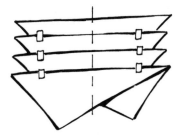

Flip the assemblage over.

Fold in about 5 inches on each side toward the center, as shown. Then fold up about 5 inches at the bottom. Fold the entire piece in half along the center. Staple edges together to close, leaving the pockets of the file on both outer surfaces.

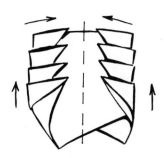

You can use both the front and back of the file.

FLASHLIGHT HOLDER
(for Working and Reading)

Make three rods, each from a *sheet* folded to page size.

Make a 1½-inch-wide straight strip from a *sheet*. Bend the rods in half. Put the rods with their unfolded edges inside the strip, about 1 inch apart. Staple the strip on both sides of each rod to keep it in place. Then wrap this strip with the rods in it tightly around the flashlight and tape closed securely.

The flashlight can be placed so that the light points either up or down. When the light is used pointing down, the rod legs can be adjusted to change the angle of light.

FLYSWATTER
(OR PUPPET)

Use four *sheets* folded together to page size.

Fold lengthwise the top down to the center.

Now fold into a long straight strip about 4 inches wide.

The heavier part at the top of the strip becomes the head of the swatter. Make cuts below this part about 1½″ in on each side.

For the handle, roll the long sides toward the center and tape together. The bottom part folds into a handle.

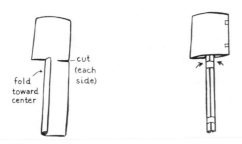

To make a bouncy puppet that children are delighted to play with, cut out triangles below the heavy fold about 1½ inches in on each side. The head jiggles and jogs as you move the handle, creating animation.

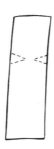

Pinch the center of the heavy fold and staple to shape the nose.

Decorate with eyes, hair, etc.

FOOTWARMERS

Use a crushed *sheet* folded to half-page size for each foot-warmer.

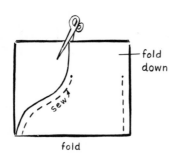

Cut out the bootee shape and fold down the top edges, as shown.

Sew all but the top edges together.

Stuff small pieces of crushed paper between the outer layers and then tape down the fold at the top.

Comfortable for one-time wear around the house or ski lodge; can also be worn as a boot liner or for extra warmth under the covers or in your sleeping bag.

FUNNEL

Fold a *sheet* to half-page size. Draw a circle 9 inches in diameter.

To hold the layers of paper together, staple inside the drawn outline, then cut out the circle.

Fold the circle in half. Make a cut to the center on the crease.

Overlap the cut edges to the size you need. Staple closed. Snip off the point at the bottom to make a hole.

You can make a colander in the same way; just crease and cut holes, as shown.

This makes a fine beach toy for sifting sand.

In the garden, use it to strain pebbles from soil.

Water will filter clean through a funnel without a hole at the bottom.

GREENHOUSE AND TOY

You'll need thirteen rolls for the toy, plus one more for the greenhouse.

For each roll use a dozen *sheets* together wrapped around a wire or string. Tape closed. The wire or string should be 6 inches longer than the roll and is used to tie the rolls together, as shown.

The structure can be flipped around in various configurations as a toy or used as a pup tent for play.

Covered with a piece of plastic, it is a portable greenhouse.

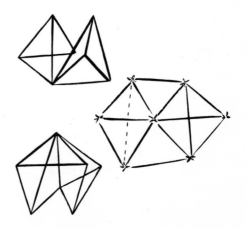

GRIPPER

Make a heavy roll from two *sheets* together. Bend in the center. Holding both ends, you can grab objects and manipulate them with good control.

Use for handling hot or soiled objects, like cans, bottles, rags. Use as an aid in lifting and pouring.

HALTER
(Kerchief)

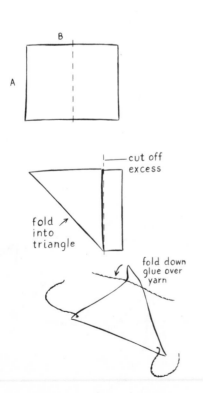

cut off excess

fold into triangle

fold down glue over yarn

Crush a *sheet* of paper. Bring one side (A) up to the top (B) and fold into a triangle. Cut off the excess.

Bend in the edges around the open sides and glue down. Lay a string of yarn across the top of the point, fold the point over and glue and tape down. Add yarn to each side at the bottom points. If you want, iron the halter to smooth out the creases.

A fine kerchief can be made using the same technique. Add paper or yarn ties to the bottom points to fasten the kerchief.

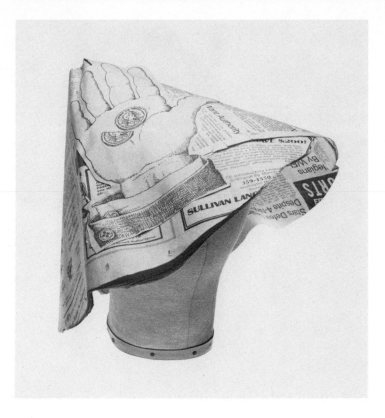

BONNET

Put three *sheets* together. Fold to quarter-page size. Cut off one corner along a curve.

Reopen to page size and starting at each side, cut on center line to within 1 inch of the middle.

Bring edges *1* and *2* of *A* part way toward the center of *B,* forming a bonnet shape. Fasten overlapped edge with staples or tape.

Use for protection against the sun. Also on a windy or rainy day —add string ties to hold it on.

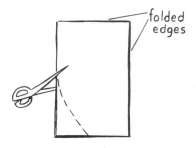

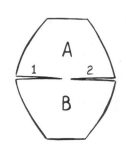

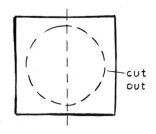

cut out

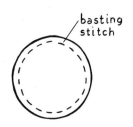

basting stitch

CAP (OR TAM)

Put two *sheets* together and crush. Smooth out. Cut a circle. Baste about ¾ inch in around the edge and gather.

Make a 1½-inch-wide straight strip from a *sheet*. Measure it to fit your head, cut to size, and staple the ends to form the band. Fit the gathered circle inside the band. Staple to hold it in place.

For the peak, make a 3-inch-wide strip from a *sheet* folded to quarter-page size. Cut as shown. Staple the wider side inside the band.

Without the peak, the hat becomes a tam.

HEADBAND

The headband is useful as an ear protector. Crush a *sheet,* fold to page size, and make a 2-inch-wide strip. Fasten string on each end for ties.

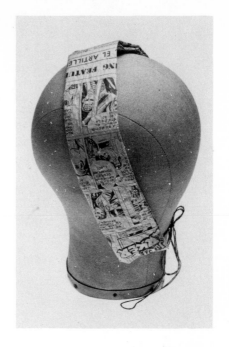

CAP LINER

To make a warm hat that can fit inside a knitted cap, crush a *sheet* of newspaper. Fold in half lengthwise. Adjust to head size and tape closed.

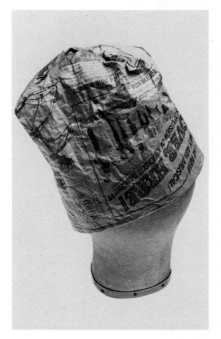

PLEATED HAT

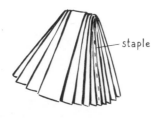

staple

Use two *sheets* together. Pleat the entire length, starting from one of the short edges.

Fold in half, bring the edges together, and staple closed along both sides.

If it is not windy, the hat will stay on just fine, but you can add braided paper or yarn ties to secure the hat if need be.

It is good as a rain hat as well as a sun hat.

SUNGLASSES HAT

Use a *sheet* folded to page size. Fold and glue as shown. Place the hat on your head. It will cover your face. Use a crayon to mark the placement of the eyeholes.

Cut out eyeholes and glue on tinted disks.

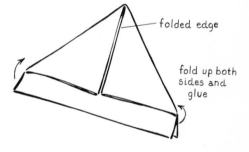

folded edge

fold up both sides and glue

ROLLED HOLDER

For pins, pencils, pens, paperclips, needles, flowers, paint brushes, toothbrushes, toothpicks (hors d'oeuvres), steel wool, nails, tools.

For each holder, use a diagonal strip made from a *sheet*. Start winding at one end to make the center of the disk. Continue to wind to the end of the strip. Tape closed. Tape over the bottom, too.

For flowers, use either immersed in water as a frog or for dried arrangements.

Use a disk made from a *page* tightly rolled into a diagonal strip as an emergency shoe heel replacement.

A disk can be made larger by adding more strips. Tape or glue them end to end as you wind.

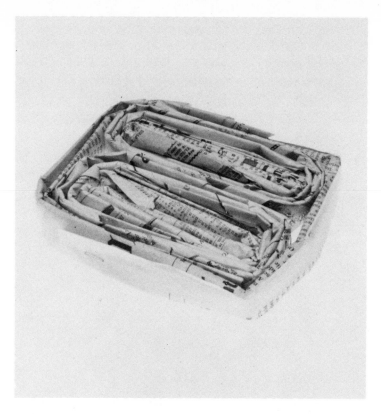

This square pad is useful not only as a hot pad, but as a trivet for plants, platters, and pots. In multiple units it can be used as a table pad. It also makes an excellent knee pad for use while doing housework or gardening.

Make five 1-inch-wide diagonal strips, each from a *sheet*. Fold one strip into 4-inch pleats and wrap a second strip around this core. Fasten with tape.

Make another unit in the same way with two more strips. Wrap the remaining strip as tightly as possible around the outside of both units to hold them in place. Tape closed.

KINDLING

Here are two kinds of newspaper kindling, both very useful. The *Nantucket kindling* gets a fire off to a faster start and is easier and quicker to make. The English-style *kindling bricks* are slow to burn and make a good hot fire starter. Use at least three.

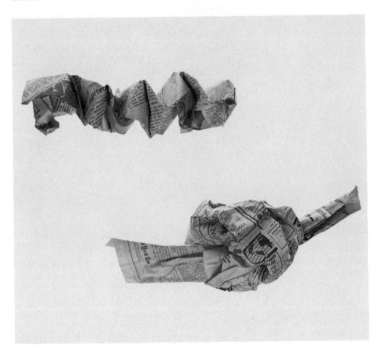

KINDLING BRICKS

For each brick use one *sheet*. Make a diagonal strip.

Fold the strip in the middle so that *A* is down and *B* to the right.

Then fold *B* over to the left.

Next, fold *A* up, then *B* back and to the right, and *A* back down.

Continue folding *B* left, *A* up, *B* right, *A* down, etc. for the full length of the strip.

Tuck in the last piece.

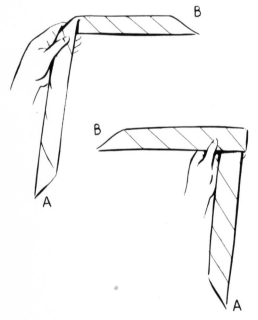

NANTUCKET KINDLING

Roll a *sheet* of newspaper very loosely on the diagonal. Tie a loose knot in the middle.

For the kindling carrier you'll need fourteen 2-inch-wide strips, each made from a *sheet* folded to page size.

Lay half the strips next to each other to make a warp.

Weave the remaining strips into the warp as shown, leaving a couple of inches unwoven on all sides.

Then, except for the handle strips, fold back these free ends and tape them down or tuck them into the woven part.

Bring together, overlap, and staple together the ends of each handle strip.

LAMP AND SHADE

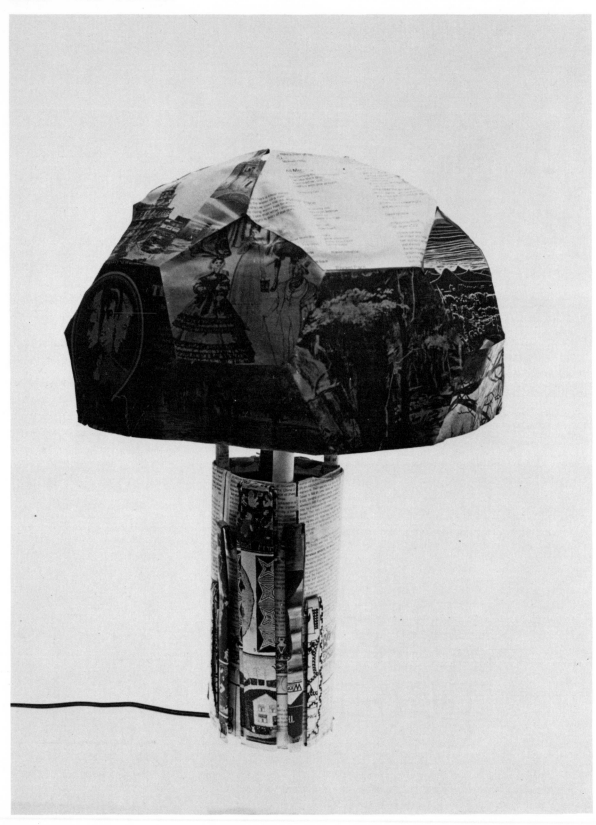

You'll need a lamp socket assembly.

For the base of the lamp, you'll need five disks. Each disk is made from four diagonal strips, each strip folded from a *sheet* of newspaper.

Start each disk by wrapping an end around the electric cord of the assembly. This places the cord in the middle of each disk.

To hold the shade on the lamp, make three rods, each from two *sheets* together folded to page size. Take 2 inches off the top of the rods. Space the rods evenly around the core of stacked disks and tape in place.

Make a 1-inch straight strip from a *sheet* folded to page size and staple the ends together to form a ring. Insert the ends of the rods, with a dab of glue on each, inside the ring; staple and tape in place. The geodesic lamp shade rests on this ring.

To make a cover for the core of stacked disks, use a *sheet* folded to one-half *sheet wide*. Wrap around the core and the rods and tape closed. Decorate with strips of different lengths.

It's easy to staple pleated paper to the top ring for a shade. For one that will last longer, make the geodesic lamp shade.

GEODESIC LAMP SHADE

Use two layers of newspaper laminated. Cut a shape twice the size for each of the patterns shown.

Cut out ten hexagons, five pentagons, and five half hexagons.

On a flat surface tape five hexagons together as shown.

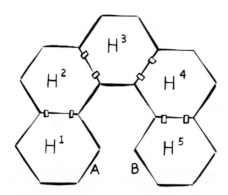

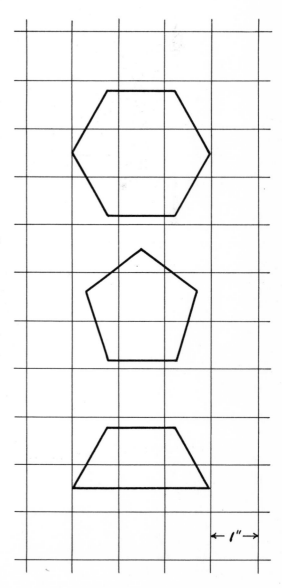

Then tape sides A and B together, thus beginning to form a rounded shape.

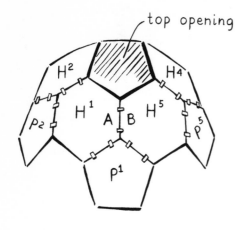

Tape five pentagons to make the next row of the shade. The point of each pentagon is taped to the bottom space between two hexagons as shown.

Tape the remaining five hexagons between the pentagons. To complete the shade fill in the bottom spaces with the five half hexagons.

Coat the shade with gesso (available at hardware or art supply stores) to stiffen it. Let dry.

For the top layer, cut the same number of forms as above from a single layer of newspaper, choosing the pictures or designs carefully. Cut each form about ⅛ inch bigger all around. Glue in place.

LOG CARRIER

You'll need thirteen *sheets* to make a log carrier. Start by putting three sheets together and overlap two sheets on top, as in the top drawing.

Follow the remaining directions, as shown.

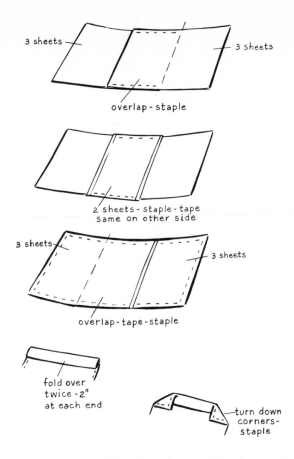

You can transport several fireplace logs or kindling easily and neatly with this carrier.

You don't have to use expensive log rollers. All you need to do to make logs out of old newspapers is to use at least ten *sheets* folded to page size. Overlap, then roll loosely and tape closed. The trick is to roll the sheets so that you get a log about 3 to 4 inches in diameter. If your finished log is much smaller than this, you've rolled it too tightly and it won't burn well.

LOGS FOR BURNING

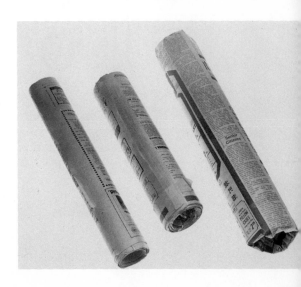

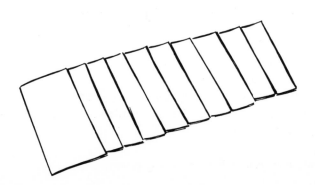

LOOM

This little loom is used for weaving strips of yarn that can be made into belts or headbands or sewn together to make an afghan.

Roll three tubes each from a *sheet* of tabloid paper folded to one-half-page size. Tape closed. (Be sure that the inner diameter of the tube is large enough for the yarn you are using.) The number of tubes you use determines the width of the woven piece, but use at least three.

Thread long pieces of yarn through each tube. Tape each at the top to the tube, then tie all together in a knot at the other end so that the weaving cannot slip off.

Tie a long piece of yarn to an end tube; start working under and over. As the weaving fills the tubes, push some down and onto the yarn that is protruding from the ends of the tubes.

When finished, cut to release the yarn from the tubes, allowing enough length for a knot at the top. The tubes can be used over and over again for many weavings.

Make marionettes from newspaper rolls of various sizes. For the one shown (directions below) tabloid paper was used.

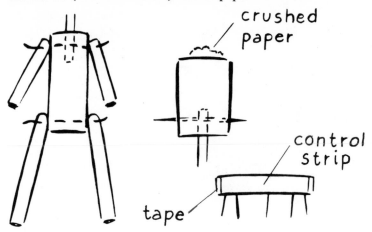

Make a roll for the body from a *page* folded into thirds. Tape closed.

Make two rolls, each from a *page* folded to one-half-page size. Tape closed. These are the legs.

Make a roll for the head from a *page* folded into quarters lengthwise. Tape closed.

For the arms, make two rolls, each from a *page* folded along the width, into thirds. Tape closed.

Make one small roll from a *quarter page*. Tape closed. This will be fastened inside the head and body to form the neck.

Add the features and body decorations before you put the marionette together.

Insert one end of the small neck roll into the head and the other into the body.

Sew the arms and legs to the body with needle and thread. Be sure to sew each arm through the neck tube.

Fasten the other end of the neck tube to the head by inserting a toothpick from one cheek, through the tube, and out through the other cheek.

Stuff the head opening with crushed paper and tape closed. Sew long pieces of thread to head, arms, and legs to make a performing marionette. Sew the threads to a strip (folded in half and taped) for easy handling.

MAT

Make twenty-four 2-inch straight strips, each from a *sheet* folded to page size.

Use one strip as a top border. Tuck ten strips inside the border strip at right angles to it, edges touching, until the groove of the border strip is filled.

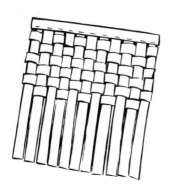

Staple in place, creating a warp.

Weave another ten strips over and under the warp strips.

When the warp is filled, add border strips at sides and bottom to cover the raw edges.

Staple in place.

Great for school use, both indoors and out.

A useful mat on a snowy or rainy day at the doorway.

You may want to cover the entire floor of your beach cottage with these mats, and they make fine groundcovers for camping, too.

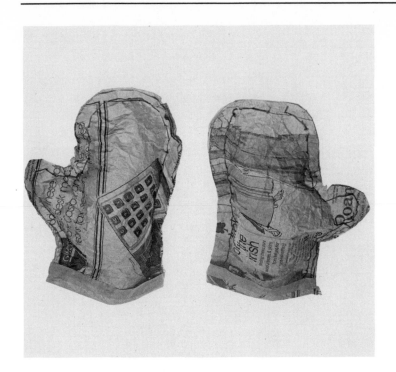

For each mitten, use a crushed *sheet* of newspaper, folded to half-page size.

Lay your hand on top and trace around it.

Cut out mitten shape with ample margin (as shown by solid line), keeping bottom opening wide to admit hand.

Fold in the cut edges and sew the mitten together, leaving the bottom edges open.

For additional warmth, stuff small pieces of crushed paper between the outer two layers; then fold and tape those two layers closed at the bottom.

Use for dirty jobs or as an insulating liner in another mitten.

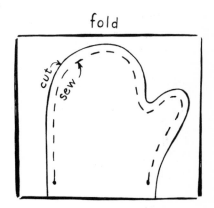

PALETTE TRAY, BRUSH, AND DRAWING TOOL

Construct a useful palette tray from eight *sheets* folded together to half-page size. Cut, fold, and tape as shown.

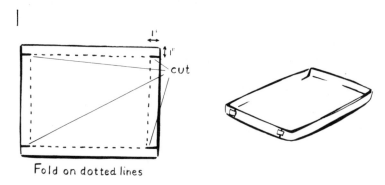

cut

Fold on dotted lines

The tray holds paint, water container, and brushes. It can be carried easily and stands firmly on the floor or on a table top.

Make small containers for paint or paste in the same way and place them inside the tray.

The brush is a roll made from a tabloid *page* folded in half and taped. It can also be used as a glue stick.

Make the fine line tool the same as a tine of a *comb,* using a tabloid *page* folded in half twice. This is a useful tool for drawing with ink or for applying liquid crayon or wax in batik work.

Use newspapers for art work of all kinds:
—painting with tempera, oil, or acrylic
—drawing with crayon, pencil, India ink, or felt-tip pen
—printing woodcuts and linoleum blocks with either water-soluble or oil-base ink

Newspapers are good for testing these media and/or for the finished work.

To make a stencil, laminate two *sheets* together, spray the surface with clear plastic varnish, and cut out your design with a knife. Use with either brush or spray. The stencil will last for many applications.

The printed pages can add texture and interest to your work.[1]

PARASOL

For the handle, use five *sheets* together. Make a diagonal roll. Tape closed.

For the stop, make two diagonal strips 2 inches wide, each from a *sheet*. Tape the end of one strip to the handle about 2 inches below the top. Roll the strip around the handle. Attach the second strip with tape to the end of the first and continue rolling. Tape closed.

For the top, pleat two *sheets* together along the width. Repeat, because you will need two of these. Fold and staple the edges together to form a round shape. To fill in the shape, use a *sheet* folded to half-sheet width, pleat as above, fold, and staple to the edges of the other pleated pieces.

Put the handle through the hole in the center of the pleated top. Tape to hold the top to the handle.

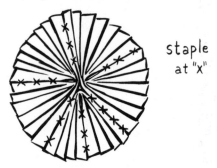

staple at "x"

PEDESTAL

Using ten *sheets* together, make a tight, firm roll. Tape closed.

Use at least eight of these rolls for a pedestal. Glue together and tape together at top, bottom, and center.

Around the center of the column, glue a 6-inch-wide strip.

For the top, roll seven or eight diagonal strips, each made from a *sheet*. Wind into a disk, adding on each strip with a little tape or glue. Push down so the sides fit on the top of the pedestal. Pat to level the top surface. Drop some glue into the crevices.

The pedestal is attractive for holding plants or sculpture.

Use two or more pedestals as table legs. Place a sturdy board across the top.

PENCIL CASE

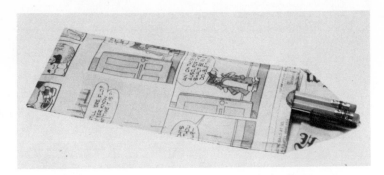

Use a *sheet* folded to page size. Fold up the bottom edge about 2 inches. Make a straight strip about 4 inches wide and fold up to within 2 inches of the top edge. Staple or tape the sides. Shape the 2-inch flap so that it can be tucked into the top opening to close.

PICTURE FRAME

Fold a *sheet* to half-sheet wide. Make a straight strip about 1½ inches wide. Keep the open side in toward the center of the frame.

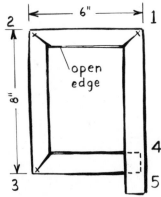

1. At about 9 inches from one end, bend the strip at a right angle, tucking in a diagonal corner as you do so. Staple the corner.

2. At 6 inches further along the strip, make another corner and staple.

3. At 8 inches make another corner. Staple.

4. Trim and tuck in the remainder of the strip to make the last side.

5. Make a corner 8 inches from the top. Trim as necessary. Staple.

For the back, fold a *sheet* to half-page size. Fold in half twice, first one way, then the other. Cut ½ inch smaller than the frame all around. Put inside the strip. On the back, tape the open edges closed.

Using a piece of paper 3 by 3 inches, fold a small flat strip. Bend into a loop. Glue and/or tape to the back of the frame for hanging. Glue small flat strips around the front opening for trim.

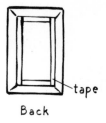

Back

Use a *sheet* of paper folded to page size. Crush it and smooth it out four or five times. Staple and tape two sides closed. Crush five half pages and stuff them into the opening. Staple and tape the pillow closed.

The pillow shown is small—ideal for use in a train, bus, or car. A large pillow can be made from two *sheets* folded to page size.

PILLOWS
(Quilt, Crib Bumper, Groundcover)

Make the crib bumper like the pillow only staple the long sides together.

If you prefer, wrap the bumper with a towel or piece of sheeting.

Make a quilt (and groundcover) by sewing small pillows together.

The quilt shown is a very warm and durable crib-size (eighteen pillows) cover.

Adding more units, you can make a quilt for a full-size bed.

Use the quilt plain or inside a blanket cover. Either way, the multiple layers of paper capture and retain the heat of the body.

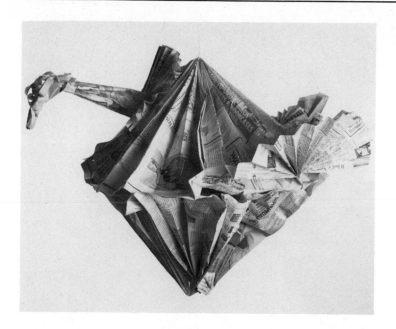

The piñata game originated in South America, where it is part of the Christmas festivities. The piñata is filled with sweets and small favors, decorated, and hung by a cord from the branch of a tree. In turn, each child is blindfolded and given a long stick with which he can strike once at the piñata. When the piñata is hit squarely, it breaks and the contents are scattered for all the children to share. The child who breaks the piñata is the hero of the day.

Put two *sheets* together and, using the full width, pleat, making each pleat about 1½ inches deep. Make four of these units.

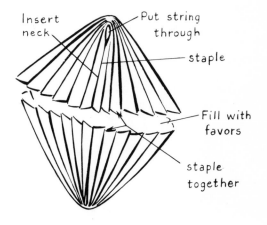

Fold and staple the sides of two units together for the top. Do the same with the other two and use for the bottom. Fill the bottom section high with candy and favors; then staple the top and bottom together all around.

Shape a loosely rolled *sheet* folded to half-page size for the neck and head. Insert into top and staple in place. Trim with tiny pleated strips and with curled thin strips.

Make small pleated semicircles, each from a half *page,* for the tail trim. Staple onto the piñata.

Put a string through the top and hang.

Make other party items such as party hats, party favors, candy containers, confetti, streamers, and newspaper loops. For these the colored pages of the comics and the Sunday magazine supplement are ideal.

HANGING
PLANT HOLDER

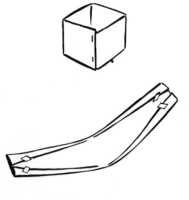

Make two strips, using two *sheets* together for each. Use the full width of the sheets to make each strip by folding in half, then in half again.

Using one strip, insert one end inside the other to about one third the length of the strip. Staple in place. Flatten; then open and shape into a square.

Taper the ends of the second strip. Tape down.

Center the square form on top of the second strip. Bring the sides of the latter over and into the square.

Use one long loop of cord. Catch it under the folds of the second strip as you turn in the sides. Staple this second strip to the sides close to the cord. Using a single loop of cord permits easy adjustment of the pot in hanging.

Roll a diagonal strip loosely from a *page* of newspaper to use as a wick. Wet thoroughly with water. Immerse one end in a jar of water and plant the other end in the top layer of soil in the pot. Keep the length of the strip as short as possible from the top of the water jar to the top of the flower pot. A quart jar of water will keep a plant moist for several weeks.

If you have many plants, you can leave them attached to one large container of water with as many newspaper wicks as you need coming from it.

PLANT LIFELINE

PLANTING POT

Fold a tabloid *sheet* lengthwise and then once again. Wrap this strip around your fingers, using a little more than half of it.

Place your palm down and fold strip as shown.

Now bring the strip around under the bottom opening and tuck the remaining part into the top of the pot.

To make the pot more leakproof, you can staple it together and tape the corners.

Seedlings grow well in this container. Water is retained by the paper for days, keeping the seedlings moist.

You don't need to transplant the seedlings. Simply put the plant and newspaper pot directly into the ground. The newspaper will eventually disintegrate and make a good mulch. The zinc in the ink protects the plant roots from grubs and other destructive insects.

PLAY UNITS

Make your child a playhouse or fort based on the structure in the photograph. With some modifications, it can also be used as a versatile storage compartment, shed, or lean-to.

Make yourself a cold frame of any size and grow seedlings or plants beneath a protective sheet of plastic. Use the structure as an enclosure for puppies and other pets.

Even young children can easily assemble their own structures from play units as they do from building blocks, and then take them apart and make something else. There are many possibilities for creative building. One child built himself an Indian tepee; later he took it apart and laid the play units along the sides of an imaginary roadway for toy cars and trucks.

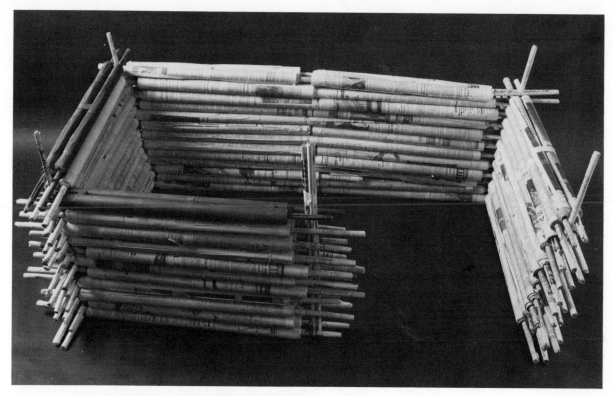

**PLAY HOUSE PARTIALLY ASSEMBLED FROM
PLAY UNITS (FLOOR SPACE 4 BY 8 FEET)**

For each basic building unit you'll need two rolls made from ten *sheets* each, two rods made from two *sheets* each, and two short rods each made from a *sheet* folded to half-page size.

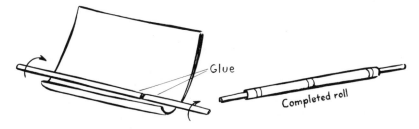

First, make half a unit. Fold ten *sheets* together to page size. Lay a full-size rod and a short rod on top and hold in place with a dab of glue. Roll the ten sheets tightly around the rods and tape closed. Several inches of rod extend from both ends of the roll.

Make another half unit in the same way and tape the two together to make a full unit.

For a long side, make units as above and then make a matching number without the short rods. Place the rod you do use in these matching units so that it extends about 6 inches from one end. Insert the rods of one end of one unit into the open end of a matching unit.

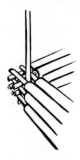

Build by laying units in alternating layers at right angles to each other. As you pile them up, the rods form a crisscross into which you can place a standing rod to stabilize the structure.

Where there is an open end (for a doorway, for example) use two rods taped together for the vertical holding pieces.

Unless you tape or glue them for permanence, log structures are easily taken apart and reassembled.

PULL TOY

For the center support you'll need two rods, each made from two *sheets* together folded to page size.

For the handles, make two rods, each from a *sheet* folded to page size. Bend each rod into a U shape, pinch its sides together, and tape to form a handle.

Make the wheels from diagonal strips rolled from a *sheet*. For each small wheel use two 1-inch-wide strips, and for each large wheel use four or five strips, each 1½ inches wide.

Make two rods for axles, each from a *sheet* folded to half-page size.

Form each wheel by wrapping the strips around your finger so that a hole is left for the axle. Tape the ends of one strip to the beginning of the next as you wrap them around. Tape the handles onto each end of the frame. Slip the axles into the frame. Wrap tape firmly around on both sides of the axle and around the center section of the frame, as shown.

Slip the wheels onto the axles close to the frame. To hold them in place use 1-inch-wide strips, each made from a *page*. Tape one end of the strip to the axle, wrap it around the axle, and tape closed.

The pull toy shown in the photograph has been decorated with cut and curled newspaper.

The toy can be pulled from either end. Attach a string if you like.

QUOITS

Quoits is a ring-toss game; you throw the quoits (rings) like horseshoes, trying to get them on the post.

To make the post, put five *sheets* together and fold to half-page size. Roll tightly and tape closed. The post shown has a cover (optional) made from a *page* folded to half-page size and rolled around the post and taped closed.

For the base of the post, roll five diagonal strips, each from a *sheet* of newspaper. Tape one end of the first diagonal strip to one end of the post and wind the strip around the post and then around itself as you would in making a disk. Add the other strips end to end, taping each to the one before.

For each ring, use a *sheet* folded to page size. Make a 1-inch strip and staple its ends together to form a ring.

RACK

A. Make five pegs. For each, fold a *sheet* to half-page size. Using the width, fold into thirds. Roll tightly and tape closed.

B. Make two straight strips, each from two *sheets* folded to page size. Using the width, fold into strips 1½ inches wide.

Lay pegs out evenly on top of one strip. Tape in place, leaving 1½ inches at each end of the strip. Fill spaces between pegs and at ends with folded 1½-inch strips (each made from a *sheet*) to height even with the top of the pegs.

Cover with the other strip. Glue and tape assemblage together tightly.

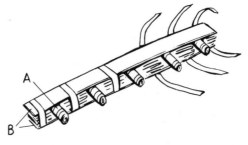

C. Make two rolls, each from a *sheet* folded to page size. Tape together.

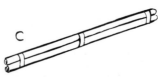

D. Make one roll from two *sheets* together folded to page size.

E. Make three straight strips, each 4 inches wide and each made from a *sheet* folded to page size.

Place roll *D* inside one strip *E* and staple the strip closed.

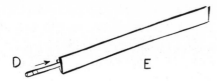

Make a hole in each of the other strips *E* to slip over the end pegs.

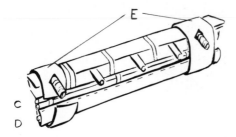

Put parts together as shown and tape the strips closed.

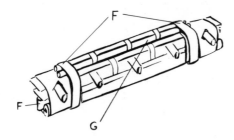

F. Make three straight strips each 1½ inches wide and each from a *sheet wide*.

Wrap one around the front over the two rolls *C*. Tape the strip in back.

Use the others to wrap around the rack between the end pegs and those next in toward the center. Tape closed.

G. Make two rolls, each from a *sheet* folded to half-sheet wide. Tape together.

Push these under the straps *F*.

Put nails between rolls *G* and the top of the rack to secure to wall.

HAND RAKE

This sturdy rake is perfect for turning over the earth in your potted plants. Also works well for gardening outdoors.

Fold a tabloid *page* to half size. Bring folded edge in to the center. Fold each side in half toward the center three more times. Bring sides together and tape closed. This is one prong.

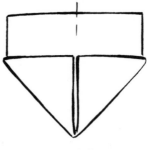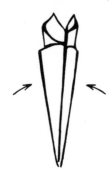

Make at least three of these.

Tape them together near one end and use that as the prong end.

You can make a prong from a strip 3 to 5 inches wide to use as a small cleaning tool.

SANDALS

THICK-SOLED SANDALS

Prepare nine diagonal strips, each made from a *sheet* rolled tightly and then flattened. Tape each strip closed with a small piece of tape. Make five straight 1-inch strips, each from a *half-page long*.

Begin to make the sole by folding down a 7-inch length at one end of a diagonal strip. Encircle this 7-inch length with the rest of the strip and tape down the end. Tape on a second diagonal strip over the end of the first and continue to encircle the center section of the sole. Tape closed. Add a third diagonal strip in the same way.

Then wrap one of the straight strips around across the middle (A) as shown, and tape this straight strip closed.

Add a fourth diagonal strip, taping one end on to the side. Start wrapping a straight strip across as shown (B). Bring the diagonal strip over the straight strip on one side and the straight strip over the diagonal strip on the other side. Tape on a fifth diagonal strip and continue to encircle, crossing with the straight strip. Tape down the end of each strip when it is fully used.

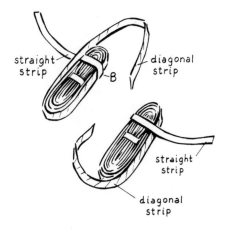

Tape on a sixth, seventh, and eighth diagonal strip in the same way, using another straight strip (C) across as shown.

At B, where the second straight strip is wrapped across, add the sandal strap. To do so, put a diagonal strip through the outer diagonal strip. Adjust the strip to fit your foot. Keeping the strip centered, bring up the sides, overlap each end to the other side, and trim. To tape the strap securely, wrap tape around the whole strap.

Wrap a straight strip tightly around across the middle (A) of the sandal. Tape closed.

Outline the finished form onto a *page* folded twice. Laminate the layers and cut out the form. Glue the cut shape in place on top of the sole.

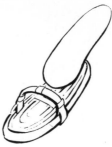

To finish, wrap a straight strip forward and back. Pull each snugly, and glue closed.

The instructions given fit a size 8. You may need fewer diagonal strips for a smaller size foot or more for a larger foot. For all sizes, however, start with the 7-inch fold, encircle diagonal strips, and use straight strips across.

THONG SANDALS

For each sole, put two *sheets* together and fold to page size.

Using the length, fold the sides toward the center and fold again to make a long narrow strip. If you need a narrower sole, adjust to size before you make the last fold.

Fold the strip in half. The folded edge is the front of the sandal. Fold the back edges in to fit the length of your foot. Staple and tape closed.

Braid a band (of straight strips of newspaper or yarn) about 25 inches long. Put it between the layers at the back of the sandal. The band is worn crossed over the back of your ankle, laced through the thong loop, and tied as shown.

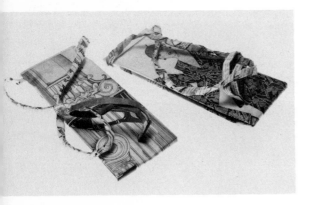

For the loop, cut a 2-inch-wide strip from the length of a *page*. Fold three times and glue closed. Place your foot on the sandal to mark the spot between your big toe and second toe. With a nail, make a hole just big enough so that the ends of the thong loop can be wedged into it and taped securely to the bottom of the sole.

Before you tape down the ends of the thong loop, try on the sandal and adjust it to the right length.

Put two *sheets* together and fold to page size. Fold the page size to a 3-inch-wide strip. Crease the strip in half to mark the center.

Wrap a piece of sandpaper about 8 inches square around one half of the strip. Staple its ends together, overlapping one edge if necessary for a snug fit.

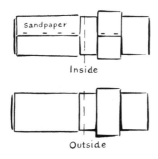

Make a 3-inch strip from a *page* folded to half-page size. Wrap this around the other half of the first strip, near the center fold, and staple its ends together, overlapping enough to allow the strip to fit around your hand.

Fold in half with the staples on the inside.

Tape the end closed.

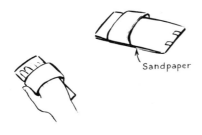

SANDPAPER HOLDER

SHELVING

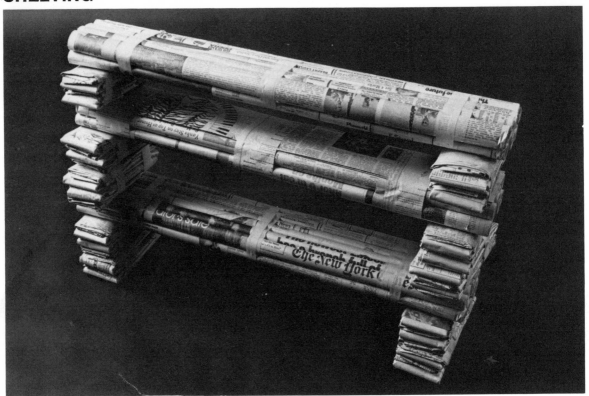

BOOKSHELVES

By attaching rolls together, you can use newspapers to support heavy weights.

In the bookcase shown, each shelf is made of two layers of six rolls each. For each roll, use three *sheets* together. Roll lengthwise and tape closed. Tape each roll to the next, then tape six together for one layer and six more together for the second layer. Glue the second layer on top of the first. Tape the double layer together.

For shorter shelves, roll the newspaper sheets along their width. Use three *sheets* together for each roll, ten rolls glued and taped together for each shelf. Since these rolls are more compact and make use of the grain of the paper, which gives added strength, one layer is sufficient.

If you make the rolls extra tight you need ten to make a single-layered shelf with the same strength as the above.

This simple use of a principle of engineering allows construction without noise or major expense.

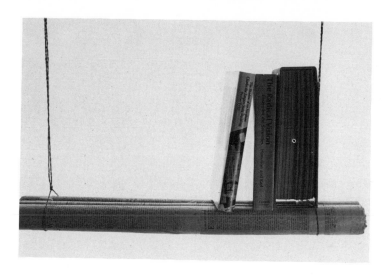

HANGING SHELF

Three rolls taped together and hung with strong cord can support heavy books, plants, radio, or knicknacks.

Make each roll from ten *sheets* stacked together. Fold to page size, roll as tightly as possible, then tape closed in several places.

SKI MASK

Laminate two *sheets*. Fold to page size and draw the pattern, as shown. Cut out and open the pattern.

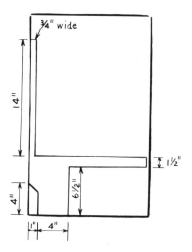

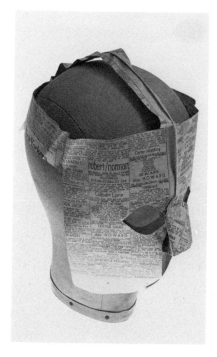

For the nosepiece, cut a 3-inch square from a single layer of paper. Fold in half to triangular shape; crease down the center. Staple the top point of the nosepiece to the mask; bring in the sides of the mask and tape the nosepiece in place.

Tape plastic disks over the eyeholes. Staple the center bottom edges of the mask together. Adjust the headbands to your size and staple closed.

Back view

The mask will fit comfortably under your ski hat. It can protect your face from desert sun as well. Decorated, it can serve as a party mask.

SLIPPERS

These easy-to-make slippers can be worn at the beach or around the house.

SINGLE-STRAP SLIPPERS

For the soles, stack twelve *pages* together. Draw an outline around both your feet on the top page. To hold the pages together, staple inside the outline at the heel, then cut out the shape.

For the straps, make a 3-inch-wide strip from a half *page* for each slipper.

Lift up about six of the pages of each sole outline. Place the strip inside the front part of the sole, adjust to size, and staple in place. Bring down the remaining layers of the sole and glue down. Bind the front edge with tape.

CROSS-STRAP SLIPPERS

For each sole, fold two *sheets* together to page size and make a long strip about 4 inches wide.

Fold the strip to half length.

Measure the length of your foot on this strip and mark the end of your heel.

Fold the strip to desired length and tape closed.

Shape the front of the slipper by tucking in each corner.

To make a strap, fold a *half-page long* to a ½-inch strip. You need two straps for each slipper.

Staple one end of each strap to the bottom layer of the sole.

Cross the straps over, check for comfortable fit, and staple their ends to the bottom layer of the sole (leaving the top layer staple-free as before).

To reinforce, tape the bottom and top layers of the soles together at the sides of each strap.

SPACE SAVER

Take five *sheets* of newspaper folded together to page size. Fold over again to half-page size and tape all around open edges to form a sturdy backing.

For each pocket, take a *sheet* folded to half-page size. Using the length, fold in about 2½ inches from each side toward the center. Fold once more in the direction of the arrows along the dotted line, as shown.

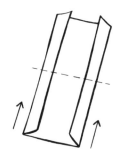

Staple finished pocket at *X* points.

Staple both pockets to backing along inside rear of each pocket, and once along top near outer side of pleat edge.

Make two holes (use awl or large nail) at the top of the backing and tie strings to hang the space saver.

Use space savers in the kitchen to hold small utensils or in closets throughout the house. Particularly useful in the hall closet for gloves and scarfs; in the bedroom for stockings, bedroom slippers, etc.

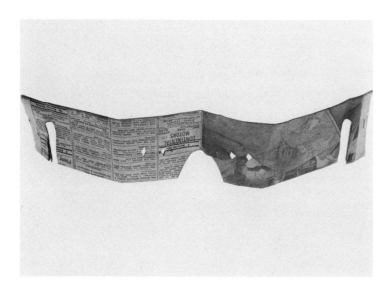

SUNGLASSES

From a single *page* folded to half-page size make a 3-inch strip. Fold in half and cut as shown.

Fold in half the long way and make very small (about 3/16 inch) triangular cuts on either side of the opening for the nose. This permits just enough light for you to see without being bothered by the sun's glare.

Without the cuts, use this as an eyeshade for afternoon naps.

TABLES

TABLE WITH LEGS

A. Legs: Lay six *sheets* each folded to page size on top of each other. Roll together tightly and tape closed. Make four of these for each leg. Glue and tape all four together.

A

B. Frame (long side): Roll ten *sheets* together tightly. Tape closed. Make a duplicate for the other long side.

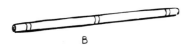

B

C. Frame (short side): Roll four *sheets* together folded to page size. Tape closed. Make a second roll. Glue and tape it to the first. Make a double unit for each short side of the table.

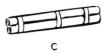

C

Assemble the four sides of the frame. Glue and tape together.

Glue the frame on top of the legs.

D. Strips for reinforcement: Make two strips, each from a diagonally rolled *sheet*. Make two more strips about 2 inches wide, using the full width of a *sheet* for each.

Glue the diagonal strips over the long sides of the table and the other strips over the short sides. Tape at the centers, corners, and around the legs.

D

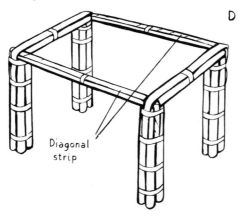

Diagonal strip

E. Table top: Use eighteen rolls, each made, using the length, from four *sheets* together folded to page size. Tape each roll closed. Glue and tape the rolls together in two sets of four each, and two sets of five each. Then tape all eighteen together and glue to the top of the frame on legs.

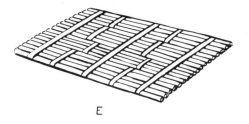

E

CUBE TABLE

Make each roll for the cube table from three *sheets* together folded to page size, rolled, and taped closed.

You need thirty-four rolls the width of the page (about 14½ inches) and twelve rolls of 12½ inches. (Cut the sheets before you make the short rolls.)

A. Glue and tape together three 14½-inch and one 12½-inch rolls, as shown, for each *A* unit. Make six units.

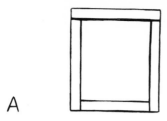

A

B. Put four *A* units together.

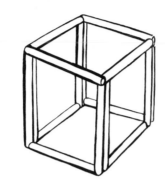

B

C. For the front and back, fill in with three 12½-inch rolls each.

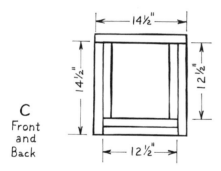

C
Front
and
Back

D. Slip one *A* unit behind each side. Glue and tape together.

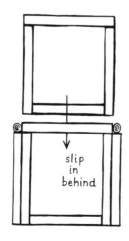

slip
in
behind

D
Sides

E. Top view of the frame.

F. Make two 2-inch strips, each from a *sheet wide*. Place on top of the sides of the frame and down the legs. Glue and tape.

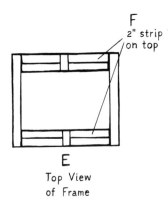

G. For the table top, use sixteen of the 14½-inch rolls. Tape four together at a time, then tape all sixteen together. Glue and tape to the top of the frame.

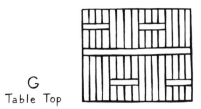

TOILET BRUSH HOLDER

We have found this holder preferable to hanging a dripping brush from a hook. And unlike the plastic holders, this one can be thrown away. However, it can be used many times before that is necessary.

Use seven tabloid *sheets* together folded to page size. Roll into a cylinder about 4 inches in diameter, and staple. Put some crushed paper in the bottom.

The tray shown is made from forty diagonal strips. Each strip is rolled from a *sheet* of newspaper.

Wind the diagonal strips tightly to make a disk, adding one strip to another. Tape or glue strips end to end. After you have rolled five or six strips, force some glue in between the strips. Continue in this way until you've used all the strips. For the final strip make two 1½-inch-wide strips folded from a *sheet* of newspaper and glue them around the finished tray. To complete the tray, make two 4-inch-wide strips. Use a *sheet* folded to page size for each. Glue these on the underside, crossed one over the other, to reinforce the tray. Trim the ends, if necessary.

TRELLIS

For the trellis use rods, each rolled from a *sheet* folded to page size.

Tape pairs of rods together at top and bottom to form the vertical members of the trellis.

Place single rods horizontally as desired by passing them between the pairs and taping them tightly to the verticals, as shown.

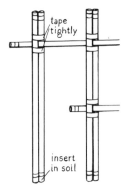

tape tightly

insert in soil

For greater strength and durability, use two *sheets* together for each rod.

The beach umbrella consists of three parts: pole, support, and top.

Pole: Make sixteen rods, using two *sheets* together for each. Tape the first two rods together, as shown. Lay the third rod in the groove created by the first two. Tape tightly to the first two. Continue to add rods, staggering each 4 inches as you lay it in the groove formed by the preceding two.

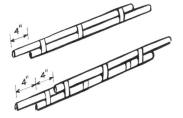

When you have added the thirteenth rod, the pole will be about 6 feet long. Shorten the remaining three rods so they fit level with the twelfth rod and tape them in place. Using a *sheet,* make a diagonal strip. Fasten it around the top of the pole at this point for the pole stop. If you want to add a finishing touch to the pole, wrap it in diagonal sheets before adding the stop.

111

Support: Make five sections, each constructed from three *sheets* together folded to page size and pleated.

Fold each in half and staple the sides together. Then assemble all five into a circle and staple together.

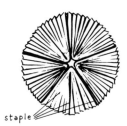

staple

Staple each pleat in two places, near the outer edge and in the middle. This adds rigidity to the support.

Sandwich the pleated circle between two single layers of newspaper, each cut from a *sheet* to fit, with a hole in the center. Glue to the top and bottom of the pleated circle.

Top: Make six rods. For each, use two *sheets* together. Using the full-sheet width, fold to a ½-inch strip. Tape closed. Cover snugly with a diagonally rolled sheet, squaring the ends as you go.

Make ten sections for the top. Each section consists of two *sheets* together. Use the full width and pleat.

To assemble, staple together in the following order, a rod, one section, another rod, two sections, another rod, two sections, another rod, one section, a rod, two sections, the last rod, and the last two sections.

Using a needle with a large eye and about 20 inches of string, sew through the pleats at one end. Pull the pleats together and tie the ends of the string.

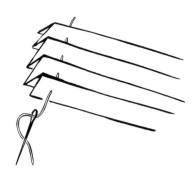

Attach the end of the last section to the first rod to complete the top.

Place the support on the pole and the top on the support.

To take the umbrella apart, you can remove the top and the support from the pole. Since the top folds closed, and the support is flat, the umbrella is easily transportable and can be re-assembled quickly.

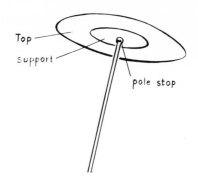

For the utility unit, make six 4-inch-wide strips, each from two *sheets* together folded to page size.

Fold each of four strips in half.

Open up each strip and bring the sides in to the middle. Tape across the open edges as shown.

Open to form a box shape.

Center the four boxes on the fifth strip and glue in place.

Glue the last strip on top. Fold the ends of the base strip up, and the ends of the top strip down. Glue both ends closed.

If you want to hang the unit, place string through one end before you glue it closed.

Horizontally the utility unit is useful singly or in multiple units for convenient countertop storage.

UTILITY UNIT

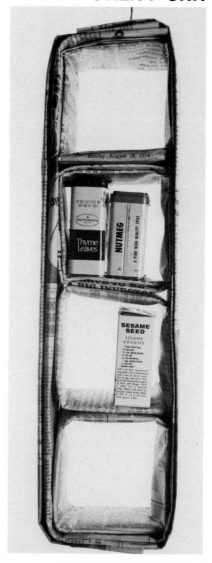

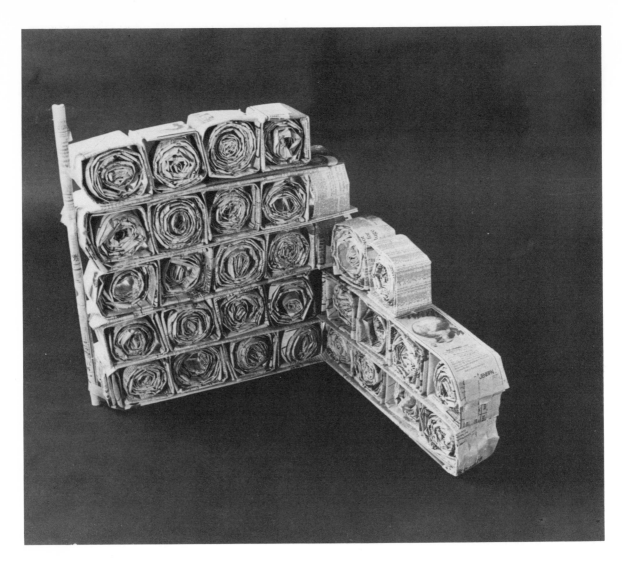

ROOM DIVIDER

Stack *utility units* one on top of the other. Glue, staple, and/or tape together.

The extra length on each base and top strip serves as a tab, allowing you to staple units together side by side for a wider construction or an L-shaped one, as in the photograph.

Make end supports from double rods and tape them along the vertical edge of the divider.

For the fillers, use rolled diagonal strips, shaped flat strips, or crushed paper.

The room divider shown stands on the floor. It can also be used on top of a chest of drawers or on a bookcase, to create a private area in a room.

Use three or four tabloid *sheets* together folded to page size. Pleat. Staple the sides together.

Make a base from a 1-inch-wide strip rolled into a round shape. Tape closed. Insert this into the bottom of the vase and glue it in place.

Make a ring to finish the base from a tabloid *half page* folded to a 1-inch-wide strip. Staple the ends together to form the ring. The bottom of the vase should fit snugly inside. Glue the ring to the vase.

You can use the vase for dried arrangements, or place a container filled with water inside for fresh flowers.

WASTEBASKET

Using a *page* folded to half-page size for each, make four rolls.

Next take a *sheet* folded to half-sheet wide. Fold and staple a 1-inch slot at the folded end.

About 9 inches on each side of this slot make another 1-inch slot.

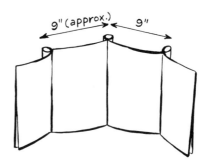

Take another *sheet* folded to half-sheet wide. Make a slot 1 inch wide down the center fold.

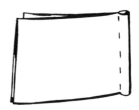

Insert a roll into each slot.

Put the second half-sheet-wide piece inside the first, as shown, and staple in place.

Make two more half-sheet-wide pieces, each from a *sheet*. Fold or trim to 9 inches. Place one across the bottom and up the sides and the other across the bottom and up the other two sides. Staple to outer sides of wastebasket.

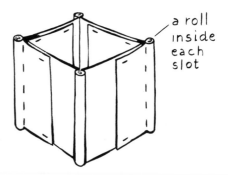

a roll inside each slot

Boots

When your boots get soaking wet, stuff them with crushed newspaper to help them dry and retain their shape.

Cane

Make a center core of three rods, each made of three full *sheets* wide. Tape together securely. Wrap the core tightly in fifteen full *sheets* wide and tape closed.

Chest Pad

Spread medication on a pad of newspapers. Place on chest to help relieve congestion.

Cleaning Aids

Shape a rolled strip around a pad of steel wool for a handy cleaning aid. Use a diagonal strip made from a *page* for the rolled strip. A plain rolled strip also works well as a scrub brush. Use a sturdy tine—made from a *page* folded to half-page size—to get dirt out of cracks and other hard-to-get-at-places.

Clothing Protection

Wrap newspapers around your sleeves and pant legs when you are doing dirty jobs.

Contamination Control

Use fresh newspapers to make a sickbed tray and to cover the bed and floor of a sickroom. Practical nurses and midwives use the center section of a new newspaper in the delivery of babies. Fresh newspaper is quite sufficiently sanitary for this purpose.

Cooling

Hang water-soaked newspaper strips in front of an electric fan to create a cool breeze on a hot summer's day.

Diaper or Mattress Filler

Use crushed newspapers to add padding.

Draining Paper

Use a pad of newspapers to absorb oil, ink, water, etc.

Emergency Heel, Knob, Wheel for Toy or Other Small Items

Use a small, tightly rolled strip. Newspaper compressed in this way makes a quick repair cheap and easy. Just tape or glue on.

Feed

"Yesterday's Newspaper Is Tomorrow's Dinner" (*Industrial Research,* April 1974). A new synthetic single-celled protein, derived from cellulose fibers found in newspapers, could alleviate the world's food problem. At least that's the hope of Louisiana State University microbiologist, Dr. V. R. Srinivasan, who has discovered a bacterium that converts cellulose into digestible protein. And in Japan some cows are maintaining good milk yield on a daily diet that includes nearly 5 pounds of old newspaper. The reading matter is mixed with molasses to provide one-sixth of their feed. This feed is cheaper than hay, which can be made only when the sun shines. University of Missouri cows are munching on algae-laden newsprint, which has a higher content of crude protein than dried beef, soybean meal, or skimmed-milk powder.

Fuel

Newspapers can be converted to methane gas, the chief component of most natural gases and a relatively nonpulluting and convenient fuel. An Indian authority, Ram Bux Singh, has shown that it is possible to manufacture small, family-sized, prefabricated, bio-gas generators that can be installed in homes as easily as a water heater. For more information regarding methane conversion in home digesters write Earth Move, P.O. Box 252, Winchester, Mass., 01890.

Groundcover for Planting

Cover seedlings with sheets of newspaper with holes cut out for the plants to grow through. This technique inhibits weed growth.

Ice Bricks and Ice Packs

Soak newspaper bricks (see *Kindling Bricks,* p. 68) or newspapers shaped to fit your needs in water and place in the freezer. Handy for picnics, parties, to place on injuries.

Insulation

Newspapers insulate well. Use where needed—on walls, in clothing, around hot or cold food. Use as a bottle warmer, to keep your pizza hot on the way home, etc. Finely shredded newspaper, fireproofed to meet building codes, can be blown into spaces between walls and floors of homes as thermal insulation. It's made by Hagan Manufacturing Company. We've been told by a user that it's easy to install and less expensive than some other insulating materials.

Litter Paper

Shred newspapers. Cats love it. Makes good nest material for hamsters and gerbils.

Mothproofing

Line closets, cabinets, and drawers with newspapers to keep the moths away. They do not like the chemicals in the paper or the ink.

Mulch

Newspapers help growing plants to flourish. Use them as a mulch around the base of a plant. They hold in the moisture and suppress weeds. Eventually the newspapers disintegrate and add to the soil's organic content. As an added benefit, the zinc in the printing ink provides a nutritional trace element and discourages harmful insects.

Packing

Protect dishes, glasses, paintings, sculpture—any delicate items in transit—with wads, rolls, or crushed sheets. Wrap them in newspapers. For plants, shape sheets of newspaper carefully around pot and plant. Tape the newspaper to hold its shape.

Paint Can Protector

Wrap a wide strip around the top of a paint can. Secure with rubber band or string. You can wipe the excess paint off your brush against this cuff.

Papier-Mâché

Use shredded newspapers to make papier-mâché. Follow the standard recipe, such as the one on p. 189 of *Paper as Art and Craft* by Newman, Newman, and Newman (New York: Crown Publishers, Inc., 1973).

Patterns

Use single *sheets* or two *sheets* laminated to make patterns for everything from clothing to furniture designs.

Plain Paper

Make your own plain gray paper from newspapers. Follow the directions given on page 15 of *Making Things* by Ann Weiseman (Boston: Little, Brown and Co., 1973).

Rags

Use plain or crushed newspapers for window cleaning, shining silver, removing nail polish, dusting.

Ripening Fruits

Wrap unripe fruit in newspaper. An old farmer's standby. Good for those green tomatoes.

Rolling Pin

Tightly roll at least sixteen *pages* together. Tape in three places. The rolling pin needs a cover: Use waxed paper for rolling pastry dough and other kitchen uses; for clay, use a newspaper cover.

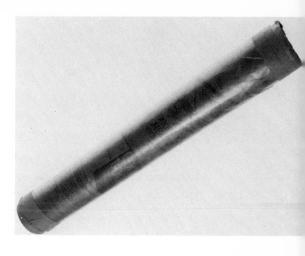

Sheaths

Fold *sheets* of newspaper to fit each knife, set of arrows, ax blade, etc. For preservation of metals, grease heavily and wrap in plastic.

Sound Absorption

Stuff crumpled newspapers into the cracks around door and window openings to seal off sound. Bags of crumpled newspaper can be used around a room to deaden the reverberation. Use pads of newspaper under noisy vibrating appliances.

Splints

Use strong rods to splint a broken limb in an emergency.

String or Yarn Holder

Make a 4-inch strip from a *sheet* folded to page size. Roll it into a cylinder big enough to hold the ball of string or yarn. Staple closed. Punch a hole ½ inch down from the top edge and thread the end of the string or yarn through it.

Table Pads

Use a pad of newspapers to protect a table top. Cover the pad with a towel for a good base for ironing.

Theatrical Scenery

Use sheets of newspaper, folded and arranged, to define space on stage or other performance area. Hang from rods or attach to side walls.

Toilet Paper

For emergency use or for camping trips, keep a supply of newspapers handy. If you crush each page three or four times and smooth it out, it will be soft and more agreeable to use. Don't worry. It will not make your fanny dirty.

Toilet Seat Cover

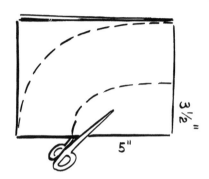

Fold a *page* in half, then fold in half again. Make a cut as shown.

Tool Handles and Covers

Use strips tightly rolled and glued to make a handle for a file or other tool. Cut out and shape newspapers to cover any tool for storage.

Tourniquet

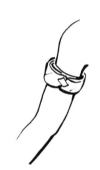

In an emergency, if there is no cloth handy, make a newspaper tourniquet. Make a diagonal roll using two or three *sheets* together. Wrap tightly around the limb and tape closed.

Typewriter Cover and Pad

Make a protective cover by shaping two *sheets* together to fit. For a pad use eight *sheets* together, folded to page size.

Wallpaper

Select your newspapers—comics for the kids, recipes for the kitchen, sports news for the sports fan—and put it up with wallpaper paste. Coat with clear plastic for durability.

Window Shade

Attach newspaper to the shade roller. Glue on additional lengths as needed. Works fine.

Wrapping Paper

Plain or fancy. In England, the famous fish and chips are sold wrapped in yesterday's newspaper. Elsewhere here and there around the world meats and other foods are handed over to the buyer wrapped in newspaper. It absorbs excess liquid and grease, and in many layers provides good insulation to keep food at the right temperature. That is the plain and practical side of wrapping. You can also use newspapers for attractive gift wrapping. Select paper carefully and use as is or with collage effects.